# With God All Things Are Possible

## 2nd Edition

### Jesus, I Trust In You

### Mark Sundy

# With God All Things Are Possible 2nd Edition
Jesus, I Trust In You
By Mark Sundy

© 2020 Mark Sundy

Printed in the United States of America

# Dedication

This book is dedicated to my beloved wife, Sylvia, who is like a Sunflower that brightens my day. To my daughter, Kristina Sundy, and my son, Nathan Sundy, who make life a joy. To my three grandchildren, Hailey, Patton, and Hunter who are my sunshine. To my future granddaughter, Mary Eleanor Sundy. To my father, Allen Sundy, and my mother, Mary Harrell Sundy, who were an inspiration to me. To the Father, the Son, and the Holy Spirit, the one and only true God—the Blessed Trinity.

# Acknowledgements

I would like to thank my sister, Rita Sundy Faulkner, for her caring support while I was working on this book.

I would also like to thank my two brothers, Randall Sundy and Steve Sundy, for their encouragement.

I am grateful to Samantha Sundy and Gary Faulkner for their support.

I also express gratitude and appreciation to Randy Chandler and Prophetic Grace Network for the prophetic word "publishing" which motivated me to finish the book that I had started six years earlier and to start publishing other books.

I would like to extend gratitude to AFM Ministries and Henry and Mary, Howard and Carolyn, Ralph and Jessica, Brenda and Steve, Freddy, Lou and Corina, Kathy and Arturo, Isidore and Donna, Lupe, and Jacque for their prayers, grace, and loving compassion.

I owe my gratitude to a multitude of Christian Mentors, Teachers, Pastors, Prophets, Evangelists, and Sunday School Teachers who helped me in my walk with the Lord Jesus Christ.

# Table of Contents

# Introduction

## With God All Things Are Possible

*But Jesus looked at them and said,* **"With men it is impossible, but not with God; for with God all things are possible."**
*(Mark 10:27, NKJV, emphasis added)*

This book is the 2nd Edition of "With God All Things Are Possible" which contains five additional Christian testimonies of God's awesome life-changing power. This book has a total of 9 Christian testimonials.

The Gospel of Mark tells us the story of a very wealthy man who approached Jesus and asked how to get into heaven (Mark 10:17-27).

A rich man came running up to Jesus and knelt before Him and asked how he could inherit eternal life. Jesus told him he knew the 10 commandments and repeated six of the commandments. The man told Jesus he had kept the commandments since he was a youth. Jesus told him he lacked one thing, then told him to sell all he had and give it to the poor. The man thought about a few minutes, then he became sad and turned and walked away. Jesus then told His disciples how hard it was for those with riches to enter the kingdom of God. The disciples were astonished and said, "Who then can be saved?" Then Jesus said, "With men it is impossible, but not with God; for with God all things are possible."

This book contains nine testimonials of God doing the impossible. Testimonials of God's redeeming power. Each of these men can truthfully say, "Jesus, I trust in You."

**And you shall know the truth, and the truth shall make you free.**
*(John 8:32, NKJV, emphasis added)*

Jesus is the truth, and the truth will make you free.

**Prayer:** *Heavenly Father, thank You for the truth of Your word the Bible. Thank You, Jesus, for the sacrifice You made on the cross of Calvary to set me free from an eternity in Hell. I give all my problems to You, God. Jesus, I trust in You! Thanks for setting me free! In Jesus' name, I pray. Amen!*

# Chapter 1

# Repeat Offender

*I can do all things through Christ who strengthens me.*
*(Philippians 4:13, NKJV, emphasis added)*

As Christians, we become over-comers through Christ who strengthens us. Donald Cannon is a man who learned to overcome through the strength of Jesus Christ.

Donald Cannon was born February 2, 1953 in Clay County, Illinois. He is currently 67 years old (2020) and lives in Abernathy, TX. Don was born with polio and wore leg braces until he was eight years old. He has four brothers and two sisters. When he was 10 years old, he and his family moved to Valdosta, Georgia. This was a big culture shock for him. He had a normal childhood and seldom got into any trouble.

He enlisted in the United States Army in 1971 when he was 18 years old.

Don did well in the U.S. Army even earning "Soldier of the Month" award. He achieved the rank of buck sergeant which is an E-5. He was in the Army airborne unit. He was stationed in Fort Jackson, South Carolina for a while. He was also in Germany for a while.

Then he was stationed in Fort Carson, Colorado in 1976. This is when everything in his life took a turn for the worse.

On Easter Sunday, he was arrested in Cartersville, Georgia for a burglary he did not commit. Don received a three-year prison sentence, but he was released eight months and 12 days later when he was found to be innocent of any crimes. The judge said he was free to go. However, Don had been dishonorably discharged from the Army in 1977 while he was imprisoned. The Georgia state prison released him at midnight in his prison uniform, and he hitch-hiked to Florida. His family had already left Florida, so he hitch-hiked back to Texas.

Don's life was never to be the same. From 1976 to 2011, Don was imprisoned a total of seven different times in three different prison systems in Georgia, Florida, and Texas. Sometimes, a repeat offender in prison is called a "knucklehead."

He was arrested for everything from stealing cars to public intoxication to assault. He did not have a problem with drugs, but he did have a problem with alcohol abuse and anger.

Don got married in 1990 after getting out of prison in Florida.

Don met his wife, Aretia, while hitchhiking through Conroe, TX in 1990. The first thing he told her was that she should not pick up strangers. Aretia said that God told her it was okay to pick him up.

This marriage changed his life for the better. His wife, Aretia, was a Christian who constantly prayed for him. Don did not have any biological children, but his wife had three daughters and a son. They became his children also. Now he has 17 grandchildren, 42 great-grandchildren, and two great-great-grandchildren. He has a good relationship with them, and they all call him grandpa.

Don stayed out of prison for 12 years from 1990 to 2002. He would occasionally get thrown into a county or city jail due to intoxication. The alcohol addiction was still a problem for him.

Don said his wife was always in church every time the doors opened, and he was always in a bar when the bar doors opened.

In 2002, Don found himself in solitary confinement with no windows in the Scurry County jail. He had been arrested for assault on Memorial Day weekend. He then went to prison for the next nine years.

Don met Jesus on May 26, 2002 while in solitary confinement at the Scurry County jail.

One night he had a vision of Jesus coming into his cell or "house" as the prisoners call it. Don said Jesus stood there in his cell and said, "If you would just be quiet, Donnie, I will make you a fisher of men."

Only his immediate family called him Donnie.

Don was given a choice, to come and follow Jesus, or continue the way he was. Don accepted Jesus and was born-again right there in his cell. The next day two other prisoners in a cell nearby said they could hear music and see lightning coming from his cell.

The other prisoners called him "Pops" which was a sign of respect because he treated everybody the same. He would often give them stamps to mail letters.

This was a life-changing experience for Don. He was immediately delivered from cussing and from alcoholism. In fact, the first thing his wife noticed that was different about him was that he stopped cussing.

Don's wife, Aretia, was a Christian, and she never gave up on him. A lot of wives divorce their husbands when they are in prison.

Don promised his wife that he would write her a letter every day while he was imprisoned. She still has the nine- or ten-year's worth of letters. In a sense, families serve time right along with the prisoners.

Don's wife brought him his first Bible while he was in the Scurry County jail in July 2002. Since that time, he has read the Bible from cover to cover a total of 43 times.

While Don was in the Scurry County jail, Danny, a church pastor from Snyder, Texas would come to visit him. The pastor challenged him to start memorizing scripture. At this point, Don had a problem memorizing anything because of the years of alcohol abuse. Don started with a short Scripture that meant so much to him.

**_Jesus wept._**
*(John 11:35, NKJV, emphasis added)*

This is the shortest verse in the Bible, but it means so much. Mary and Martha had sent for Jesus after their brother Lazarus had died.

When Jesus arrived, he seen Mary and Martha and other Jews weeping.

Jesus was moved with compassion and wept.

Don felt that Jesus wept over him all the years he was imprisoned.

It took seven days for Don to memorize the shortest verse in the Bible which contained two words, Jesus wept." This was because his memory was impaired due to alcohol abuse. However, Jesus started a process of healing Don's memory. The next week Don memorized the whole chapter of Psalm 23. Now, he has read the Bible all the way through many times, and probably knows as much about the Bible as a lot of people who have graduated from a Seminary.

From the Scurry County jail, he went to prison in South Texas, then came back to West Texas to the Wallace unit and the Dick Ware unit in Colorado City, TX.

Don hated working in the kitchen, so guess what was his first job in the Dick ware unit? Yes, he was assigned to the kitchen. His first job was to cook 1,200 pieces of fish. This brought back to his memory that Jesus was going to make him a fisher of men.

Don was paroled from prison in October 2011. Jesus changed his life, and Don has not been incarcerated again.

Don got involved in a prison ministry called "Freedom in Jesus Prison Ministries." This ministry visited him while he was in prison. "Freedom in Jesus Prison Ministries" was founded by Don Castleberry and is headquartered in Levelland, Texas. Don has been active in this prison ministry since he was paroled from prison nine years ago. This Ministry helped Don adjust after he was paroled.

Don now goes to prisons in Texas to minister and witness for Jesus Christ. Don can now do "all things through Christ who strengthens him."

Life still had its struggles. Don went to one Baptist church after he was paroled but did not feel very welcome because the pastor told him "convicts never change."

When Don preaches in prisons, he does not talk about politics or theology or even religion. He preaches Christ and Christ crucified. He tells people what Christ has done for him.

Don trusts in the Lord. He likes the acronym F.A.I.T.H. which stands for "**F**inal **A**nalysis **I** **T**rust **H**im."

Don's mom did not talk to him the last 12 years of her life. She did not want anything to do with him. Don wanted to reconcile with his Mom, so he had his wife, Aretia, send her flowers repeatedly, but to no avail.

After Don became a Christian, he became concerned about his mother who was not a Christian. He told God that if he would only save his mother, he would read a book every day out of the Bible. The King James Bible contains 66 books. After 65 days, he had read 65 books. The next day he would be finished with the last book of the Bible.

He got the news that his mother died on the 65th day. Don firmly believes that God did save his mother before she died.

Don's dad accepted the Lord and became a Christian. He died in 1992.

Don prayed for his grandkids while he was imprisoned. Don had a great grandson that was born with a condition called hydrocephalus also known as "water on the brain." He was miraculously healed in August 2004.

Jesus called Don to preach the gospel and to be a fisher of men. Don said yes and has been preaching about Jesus since 2011.

One of Don's favorite scriptures is found in Isaiah.

*The Spirit of the Lord God is upon Me,*
*Because the Lord has anointed Me*
*To preach good tidings to the poor;*
*He has sent Me to heal the brokenhearted,*
**To proclaim liberty to the captives,**
**And the opening of the prison to those**
**who are bound...**
*(Isaiah 61:1, NKJV, emphasis added)*

Don believes if he had said no to Jesus in his cell that night that he would probably be dead and in Hell by now.

He had a quadruple CABG (coronary artery bypass graft) in 2019. He came through the surgery fine, and he was out of the hospital in record time.

Don continues to proclaim liberty to the captives, and the opening of the prison to those who are bound.

He has a powerful testimony of the redeeming, restoring, and healing power of our wonderful savior, Jesus Christ!

This is also a powerful story of how the prayers of a Christian wife, and her choice to stand by her husband can change someone's world.

**Don Cannon can truthfully say, "Jesus, I trust in You!"**

**Prayer:** *Heavenly Father, thanks for setting the captives free. Thank you, Lord, for Your presence in the prisons and Your presence in the churches. Give me an obedient heart. Forgive me of my pride and doing everything my own way. I submit to you, O God! I want to follow your commandments and be faithful to You, O God! In Jesus' name, I pray. Amen!*

**Don in the Army at age 18.**

Don Cannon at age 38.

Don at age 64 with his wife, Aretia.

## Chapter 2

## Two Life Sentences

*Therefore if the Son makes you free, you*
*shall be free indeed.*
*(John 8:36, NKJV, emphasis added)*

Jose Angel Narvais is currently 60 years old
and lives near Lubbock, Texas. He owns two
auto body shops that he and his son operate.
He owns a third shop that he rents to a
mechanic. It's hard to believe that at one time,
Joe was in a prison cell serving two life
sentences.

Joe was born in Lamesa, Texas on May 17,
1960. He has two brothers and three sisters. He
is married to Birdie. Joe has three children and
11 grandchildren. His children grew up while he
was imprisoned. He was imprisoned three times
in Texas.

He was a grandpa when he got out of prison.

Joe's dad was imprisoned three times. He was imprisoned once for three years for having a small matchbox with drugs in it. Joe was five years old when his dad got out of prison.

Joe remembers his father telling him, "You won't be a man until you go to prison." The seeds for prison were planted exceedingly early in his life. Joe remembered his uncles were in the Army during the Vietnam War. They did not get much respect. People called them baby killers. Joe noticed people treated his dad with respect after he got out of prison. Joe wanted to be just like him. Joe wanted to be tough and respected just like his dad.

Joe started getting in trouble at the age of 13 years old. He lost count of how many times he was sent to the youth detention center in Lubbock, TX.

He set the car on fire of one of the teachers he did not like. He also set a desk on fire of one of the teachers he did not like.

When he was 15 years old, he started stealing cars and selling them. Then he started trading the stolen cars for drugs and selling the drugs.

He was arrested at 18 years old and went to prison for the first time at 19 years old for stealing cars, selling dope, and hitting two men with an axe.

He received an eight-year sentence and was paroled after four years.

Joe learned a lot of bad things in prison. He learned how to hurt people. Prison was like a university for learning crime.

Other prisoners would tell him to go see this guy or that guy when he got out of prison, and they would pay him to kidnap somebody or to hurt somebody.

After he was paroled the first time, he allegedly started buying drugs in Mexico and selling them here. He made a lot of money the next three years. However, the law caught up with him, and he was arrested for selling drugs and received a 10-year prison sentence. Then he started selling drugs in prison.

He was paroled after six years. Joe was only out of prison for one week when he started selling drugs again. He allegedly had 23 people selling drugs for him. Joe loved the money and power he got from selling drugs. He used to intimidate people to get them to sell drugs for him.

It was during this time that he started buying cars and fixing them up.

Joe and his brother-in-law got into a quarrel. His brother-in-law set him up by planting drugs in his house and turning him in to the cops. The cops raided his house and found the drugs.

Joe was arrested for the drugs and was accused of trying to shoot his brother-in-law.

He was also accused of organized crime and being a habitual criminal.

By this time, the judge was tired of seeing him in his court. Joe received two life sentences from the judge.

When he went to prison the third time, the release date in his records said 99/99/9999. This meant that he would never be released.

He went to a maximum-security prison called the Eastham Unit in Lovelady, Texas. It had the reputation of being the toughest prison in Texas. This prison was nicknamed "The House of Pain." This prison was built in 1930 and housed such prisoners as Clyde Barrow and Pretty Boy Floyd.

Joe stated. "An October 6, 1986 issue of *Newsweek* magazine described Eastham as the most dangerous prison in America. Knifings and beatings were common. The guards were vicious and played both ends of the game."

When Joe first arrived at the prison, he had a meeting with the warden. The warden said, "Boy, you bought yourself a lot of time. You are never getting out of here. If you mess up here, you will be put in a 4-foot x 8-foot solitary cell."

He worked in the laundry while at this prison. Joe also hustled and made money in prison. Joe was getting meaner, and his heart was getting harder every time he came to prison. Prison was becoming his home away from home. He knew how to survive in prison. Joe stated, "I was a convict, not an inmate."

Joe's old girlfriend, Birdie, came to visit him once. Joe said to her, "Don't ever come back. I cannot do time with a woman." She told him she loved him. Again, he told her not to come back.

Joe started a committee to get everyone out of gangs in the prison. That started a war in the prison. Joe was set up and attacked by gang members. He stabbed two gang members in self-defense, and he threw a third one across a steel table. To this day, there are no more gangs at Eastham. No one can claim gang membership.

While at Eastham prison, Joe was able to attend a preaching service given by a prison ministry.

There were 5000 inmates at Eastham, but only 500 seats were allowed for the preaching service. Miraculously, he was able to attend the crusade.

During the service, this "long-haired hippie dude" from California gave his testimony. He had two life sentences but was released from prison. That got Joe's attention!

Joe asked him, "How did you get out?"

He replied, "Jesus!"

Joe said, "Who was your attorney?"

He replied, "Jesus!"

Joe said, "But really, how did you get out?"

He replied, "Jesus!"

This "long-haired hippie dude" told Joe, "You have to have Faith, and Faith comes from hearing the word of God. You need to start saying, "Any day now I will get out of prison and stay out of prison." Joe began saying this every day. Joe began to realize that you can speak blessings or curses with your mouth. He started speaking blessings over his life.

Joe started reading the Bible every day. He started saying, "I am going home" every day. Joe got very frustrated because it seemed like no progress was being made. Joe just kept saying, "Any day now."

One day, when Joe was in the "hole," he got down on his knees and with tears in his eyes, he gave his life over to Jesus Christ. He was born-again that day in his prison cell. While he was praying, he started "speaking in tongues." From this day forward, everything in Joe's life began to change for the better.

One of Joe's favorite scriptures became:

**But seek first the kingdom of God and his righteousness, and all these things shall be added to you.**
*(Matthew 6:33, NKJV, emphasis added)*

Joe started trusting in God on a daily basis. He started recognizing that God was working in his life. He was transferred to a maximum-security prison in Abilene, Texas.

His family from Lubbock was able to visit him more often now.

God started transforming Joe into the person that God had destined him to be. Joe did not get into any trouble at prison for the next six years.

Joe started writing articles that were published by prison ministries such as "Convicts for Christ" and "Inmate journal."

He also published some articles in the prison newspaper called "Echo." These articles were against drugs and gang activity. Here is an excerpt from his article called "An Angel's Tear."

*"I finally fell asleep without even thanking God for getting me through another day of struggling and tired of prison life. That was a bit different for me. I had a dream as I lay there of an Angel. Yes, an Angel. This Angel seemed to be very ill or in some sort of pain. The Angel looked as if he had gotten into a fight. His wings were all bandaged, ripped, torn, and bruised all over. It seemed the Angel was very tired, barely lifting his head up as I drew closer to see what could be wrong.*

*The Angel looked at me like he lost hope or was in despair. I noticed that there was a gleam in his eyes, a sparkle that shined from within. I asked the Angel, "What is wrong or could be bothering you?" The Angel looked at me with tears in his eyes, but somehow, he smiled. "Do you not know what is wrong?"*

*And then I asked the Angel, "Who did this to you?"*

*The Angel answered, "You did this to me, Joe. Do you not know that I am your Guardian Angel?" I was startled at first. It took me a while to answer back, "Not me Angel, I could never have done this to you." The Angel said, "Yes, you did this to me, Joe. You, Joe, have lived a wild, crazy, and rough life. And you are quite a task for me. Do you not see that each bandage in my wings and the scars I have are a different story of how I protected you from harm and danger!"*

When Joe went before the parole board, the lady on the board asked, "What made you change?"

Joe said, "Jesus!"

The warden said that Joe was a holy roller and a Bible thumper.

Afterwards, the lady on the board asked Joe if she could talk to him for five or ten minutes. This turned into a 45-minute discussion. She wanted to see the articles he had written that were against drugs and gang activity.

She called Joe by his name which shocked him. It almost made him weep because the persons on the parole board normally called him by his number "386644."

Joe asked the lady, "Does this mean I'm getting out?"

She said, "Yes, in two years if you do not have any minor infractions or major infractions."

Joe was paroled two years later June 12, 1995. Joe said he cried like a baby the day he was paroled. He gave Jesus all the credit!

Jesus had done the impossible. A man with two "Life Sentences" was freed by Jesus to preach the gospel of Jesus Christ.

After he was paroled, he went to live with his mother for a short time. His mother had prayed for him all the years he was in jail. She always told Joe to have faith.

Joe's mother said, "What are you going to do now?"

Joe said, "I am going to work."

Joe's mom said they could make homemade tamales and sell them. Joe went from selling drugs to selling tamales. After Joe had been out of prison for one month, he went to the store to buy the ingredients they would need to make the tamales.

He was bending over to get one of the ingredients for the tamales when a lady come up to Joe and asked him, "Do you know who I am?" Joe did not recognize her at first, but it was his old girlfriend. Her name was Birdie. She recognized the taboo on his forearm.

Birdie was going through a divorce at the time. After the divorce, Birdie and Joe rekindled their romance. They have been happily married for 15 years now. Birdie had become a Christian and was involved in prison ministry.

She was praying for Joe while he was imprisoned. His mother also prayed for him while he was imprisoned.

The prayers of a praying mother and a praying wife are so powerful.

Joe and his wife are currently involved in prison ministries such as "Freedom in Jesus Prison Ministries" and "Road to Restoration." He has also been involved with other prison ministries called "I am Redeemed" and "Unchained."

Joe also mentors' people who are getting out of prison to help them adapt to living in the world again.

Joe also started making money by doing odd jobs like mowing grass.

He got into a car accident when a lady hit him from behind. He took his car to an auto body shop to be repaired. Joe ended up buying this body shop. He also bought a second body shop and manages them along with his son. Joe has a third shop that he rents to a mechanic. Joe has become quite successful! He gives Jesus all the credit!

Joe has recorded his testimony and put it on YouTube.

He also did a five-minute interview that was recorded by Joyce Meyer Ministries and was posted on her website.

Joe's favorite book beside the Bible is "Battlefield of the Mind" which was written by Joyce Meyer.

Joe served thirteen years and eight months of his two life sentences.

Joe was imprisoned three times and served a total of 23 years and eight months.

Jesus has turned Joe's tears of grief in prison to tears of joy. He runs a successful body shop business, has a loving wife, and has a good relationship with his children and grandchildren.

Joe and his wife, Birdie, witness and preach and teach in prisons through "Freedom in Jesus Prison Ministries" and other prison ministries.

Joe and Birdie also have their own prison ministry called "Cross to Freedom," P.O. Box 1131, Lubbock, TX, 79408."

Joe gave his life to Jesus in prison and Jesus has given Joe a new life!

Joe stated, "The most exciting part of this whole God story is that good-looking little girl that liked the show cars, the lifestyle, and the money I was flashing around as a drug kingpin. The same girl I told do not ever come back. I cannot do time with a woman. She is now my wife, and we get to go to prisons together and tell of the loving and forgiving Father we both serve. She is my very best friend in this world. Only God could do that."

**Joe Narvais can truthfully say, "Jesus, I trust in You!"**

**Prayer:** *Heavenly Father, thank You for redeeming Joe's life. Thank You for being there when Joe needed You. Thank You, Jesus, for the tears of joy that You have given to Joe and his wife, Birdie. In Jesus' name, I pray. Amen!*

Joe and his wife, Birdie.

Joe with his Mom and Dad when he was
released from prison.

Joe and his son.

Joe in prison.

## Chapter 3

# Jonah

**But Jonah arose to flee to Tarshish from the presence of the Lord...**
*(Jonah 1:3, NKJV, emphasis added)*

God told Jonah to go to Nineveh to cry out about the wickedness of that great city. Jonah did not want to do this, and he fled by ship to Tarshish. There came a great storm, and he was thrown overboard into the sea by the men on the ship. Then the storm calmed. The Lord had prepared a great fish to swallow Jonah, and he was in the belly of the fish for three days and three nights. The great fish vomited Jonah onto dry land at the command of the Lord.

For the second time, the Lord told Jonah to go to Nineveh and preach his message. Jonah obeyed the Lord this time.

Craig Daugherty is a modern-day Jonah.

Let us examine his story. Craig was born December 19, 1965 at Patrick Air Force Base. He has one brother and one sister. Craig is married and has two children. His Dad was in the Air Force for six or seven years.

He had a typical childhood until he entered his freshman year in High School in Houston, TX when he was 14 years old. A friend approached him at his locker and told him he was having a really hard day and needed to talk to him. Craig told him he was sorry he was having a bad day and hugged him. They lived 15 miles apart and Craig's only way home was to catch the school bus, or he would have to walk home. Craig told him that he was going to be okay, and he would talk to him the next morning.

The next morning on September 25, 1980 when Craig got to school, the school announced that his friend had "passed away." The next day, he found out that his friend committed suicide. Craig's friend had hung himself in his bedroom closet.

When the school made this announcement, another kid started laughing. Craig punched him and knocked him out.

He was sent to the office to talk to the school principal. After he explained why he hit the other kid, the principal said he understood.

Craig was mad at God after his friend committed suicide. He thought there must have been some way that God could have stopped this from happening. For a while, Craig did not want to have anything to do with God or church.

The other kids started calling Craig "dummy". Craig moved to Coppell, TX and finished his junior and senior at the Coppell High school. Craig went through high school isolating himself. He had put himself in a self-imposed prison.

The rest of his time in high school was very dark for Craig. He began having problems with depression and loneliness. He became a loner, and he did not want to open up to anyone.

He never kept in touch with anyone from his high school. He never cared to know anything about any of his classmates. He never wanted to attend any of his class reunions.

Craig went on to the University of North Texas after he graduated from high school.

This university had the reputation of being the second most partying university in the USA. It is ironic that he was introduced to Jesus while attending this university.

Craig's friend in college was really into Jesus. His friend was always inviting him to church and Bible studies, but he never went because he was still mad at God. His friend shared the Gospel with Craig many times, but Craig would try to argue about it. His friend never got mad at him. His friend was always kind and gentle.

Craig got drunk for the first time while a freshman in college. The room started spinning every time he laid down. Craig's friend walked with him all night around the college campus, and he shared the Gospel of Jesus with him all night. It was after this night that Craig started to believe that God might be real. This was the first "chink" in the hard armor that Craig had put around his heart.

Craig continued to think about God during the Spring semester at college. By the end of the semester, Craig gave his life and heart over to Jesus Christ.

He became a member of the Mayflower Congregational Church in Flower Mound, TX until he finished college. He joined this church because it had mostly elderly members.

Craig had started sensing that God was calling him to youth ministry, and Craig did not like teenagers. This was probably a carryover from his dark days as a teenager in high school. Craig thought "God, you are wrong about calling me into youth ministry."

Craig graduated from University of North Texas with a Bachelor of Science degree in December 1988.

After college, Craig joined the Navy because he was running from the call of God on his life.

Just like Jonah ran from God's call and fled to Tarshish, Craig ran from God's call to youth ministry and fled to the U.S. Navy.

He went to the Navy Officer Candidate School in Newport, Rhode Island in February 1989. He graduated four months later and was commissioned an "Ensign" in the United States Navy. Then he spent six months training in the Naval Supply School in Athens, Georgia.

Craig was stationed at the Naval Air Station Sigonella in January 1990 in Sicily, Italy. Craig thought this was great. He would be far away from God's calling as a youth pastor. God works in mysterious ways. Craig thought he was running from God, and the whole time he was running right into God's hands.

A youth ministry called "Military Community Youth Ministry" had started at the Naval Air Station three months before Craig had arrived for duty.

Craig met Dave who was involved with the youth ministry. Craig started getting involved with the youth ministry and was asked to speak about suicide and his anger toward God.

After he got the first sentence out, Craig wept for the first time about his friend's suicide. That was a big healing moment for him. It had been almost ten years since his friends' suicide. He finally let it go and let God be in control.

Craig loved the Lord again and knew that God had always been there for him. Craig finally realized that God was not to blame for his friends' suicide.

Craig got incredibly involved in youth ministry and now, he loved it.

He was discharged from the Navy in January 1993.

He attended Dallas Theological Seminary for two years and earned a Master of Arts degree in Christian Education. He has been youth pastor for several churches. He is currently co-pastor of Ransom Canyon Chapel in Ransom Canyon, TX.

Jesus set Craig free from his self-imposed prison of loneliness, depression, and despair.

**Craig Daugherty can truthfully say, "Jesus, I trust in You!"**

**Prayer:** *Heavenly Father, thank You for setting Craig free from despair and loneliness. Thank You for watching over Craig his whole life. Give me an obedient heart. Forgive me of my pride and doing everything my own way. I submit to you, O God! I want to follow your commandments and be faithful to you, O God! In Jesus' name, I pray. Amen!*

Craig in 1985 while a Freshman at University of North Texas.

Craig in June 1989 upon commissioning as a
U.S. Navy Supply Corps Officer.

Craig in 2017 with his family. Wife (Stacey), Daughter (Mallori), and son (Randy).

Craig in 1996 at a midwinter retreat in Majorca,
Spain with other military youth ministry staff.

# Chapter 4

# The Eagle Has Fallen

*Those who live only to satisfy their own sinful nature will harvest decay and death from that sinful nature. But **those who live to please the Spirit will harvest everlasting life from the Spirit.***
*(Galatians 6:8, NLT, emphasis added)*

In October 2019, I stood at the Houston National Veterans Cemetery as a three-gun salute was offered up in honor of my friend, Freddie Rios. He told me many stories of his days in Vietnam.

Alfred Rios was born January 15, 1948 in Galveston, Texas. He died on October 15, 2019 in Houston, Texas from the long-term effects of Agent Orange (a defoliant used in Vietnam).

He was 71 years old when he died. He went by the name of Freddy.

He was one of the most decorated soldiers in the Vietnam War.

In 2007, he was classified as 100% disabled by the Veterans Administration due to the effects of Agent Orange on his nervous system and lungs.

I met Freddy at AFM ministry in 2014 in Shallowater, TX. He was a lay minister at AFM. He was a kind gentleman, and we became good friends.

He told many stories of his days as a soldier in Vietnam. He walked with a cane due to the harmful effects of Agent Orange on his nervous system. He was exposed to Agent Orange in Vietnam where it was used to defoliate (kill) the jungle vegetation.

Freddy was a Vietnam War hero. He received over 30 citations for bravery and valor during the war. Freddy was nominated for the nation's highest military award which is the Congressional Medal of Honor. He was not awarded this medal, but he was awarded the second highest medal, the Distinguished Service Cross.

Freddy was awarded the Distinguished Service Cross for showing bravery and valor when the North Vietnamese soldiers threw a hand grenade in his foxhole. He disregarded his own life and jumped on top of the hand grenade to protect the lives of the other soldiers in the foxhole.

The grenade did not go off when he jumped on it, so he grabbed the grenade and threw it back out of the foxhole where it went off in the air and no one was hurt.

Then he jumped out of the foxhole charging the enemy. He killed two of the enemy and scattered the rest. Freddy was a sergeant that cared about the soldiers that were under him.

Freddy received two Purple Heart Medals for wounds received in Vietnam.

The first Purple Heart was awarded when he was shot through the calf muscle in the leg by a North Vietnamese soldier. Freddy said he got over that wound fast, and it really did not hurt that much.

The second Purple Heart was awarded to him when he was shot through the lungs. The bullet fragment lodged extremely near his heart. He said this wound was incredibly painful. He said the doctors were unable to remove it because it was so close to his heart.

Freddy also had shrapnel wounds in the knee, the leg, by his right eye, and on his right wrist.

Some of his other awards for bravery and valor included the Silver Star, the Bronze Star, the Army Commendation Medal, the Presidential Citation, the Infantry Badge with cluster, and three Vietnamese citations.

Freddy had over 30 metals and citations for his heroic behavior in Vietnam.

Freddy donated all his awards, metals, and citations to a museum somewhere in the greater Houston Metropolitan area.

Freddy told me one time that he loved the Vietnamese people, that they were very sweet, and he didn't mind fighting for their freedom.

Freddy was 19 years old in July 1967 when he found himself in the jungles of Vietnam.

Had completed Army Airborne Ranger training and Army Tank training. He also spent 6 months training in the jungles of Panama. He had to live off the land, and he ate a lot of dried grasshoppers. He tried eating grub worms but just could not stomach them.

By September 1967, he was in the firefight of his life. His unit was sent to a battlefield near Da Nang to help some Marines who were pinned down and being overrun. In this battle, Freddy was hit by shrapnel above his right eye, his right leg, his left knee, and other places. He was sent to a military hospital in Kentucky for surgery and recuperation.

After he recuperated, Freddy volunteered to go back to Vietnam. He was in Vietnam during the 1968 TET Offensive by the North Vietnamese.

It was during this time that he was in a battle that he jumped on a live hand grenade to save his men, and Freddy was awarded the Distinguished Service Cross.

A movie came out in 2002 called "We Were Soldiers" starring Mel Gibson about the Vietnam War. It was based on a book by Lieut. Gen. Hal Moore and reporter Joseph Galloway. It was about the battle of La Drang on November 14, 1965. The Americans engaged a much larger Vietnamese force and were almost massacred, but the U.S. Air Force was able to drive back the North Vietnamese.

A very similar engagement with the enemy came three years later on May 27, 1968 called the "Battle of Valley 506." This was the second largest engagement of the Vietnam War.

Sgt. Freddy Rios and his men of the first Battalion, 50th infantry, 173rd Airborne Brigade were sent to the Valley to engage the enemy.

The American forces numbered 800 while the North Vietnamese soldiers numbered about 15,000. Freddy told me when he first got to the Valley, it looked like a tropical paradise with flowers and the lush green vegetation.

The next day, after the battle, the beauty of the valley was gone. The scent of the beautiful flowers had been replaced with the gasoline odor of the napalm. Everything was red with blood or was blackened and charred by the napalm.

Freddy and his men engaged the enemy all day, but they were surrounded and had to pull back when darkness came. He radioed for air support, and they saved their lives by dropping napalm bombs so close to them that the hairs on their heads and arms were scorched. Napalm is a highly flammable sticky jelly used in incendiary bombs and flamethrowers, consisting of gasoline thickened with special soaps.

Through the night he could hear the screams of men wounded and then he would hear a gunshot and the screaming stopped.

The next morning, he only had a few men left. This memory brought about much emotional pain for Freddy. He always wept at this point when telling his story because of the memory of his friends who died. Freddy was awarded the "Silver Star" after this battle.

Freddy got through the Vietnam War, and he came back to United States. When he landed at the airport in California, there were protesters outside who spit on him and called him "baby killer" as he walked out of the airport.

He owned a successful publishing company, and he was making a lot of money.

He was also on the Board of Directors of a bank.

Freddy put his brother in charge of the company. Freddy started travelling and living it up. He was partying and running around with women.

However, Freddy's brother committed some illegal acts with the company financially, and Freddy took the blame for it.

Freddy ended up getting arrested and serving a two-year sentence in the Federal Prison in Big Spring, Texas.

The first day he was in prison, two tough-guy inmates jumped him. They did not know who they were messing with. With his hand-to-hand combat training, Freddy easily defeated these two numbskulls. Nobody else messed with Freddy the rest of his two year stay in the Big Spring Federal Prison.

It was during this time that Freddy started getting serious with God. Freddy gave his life to Jesus, and Jesus turned his life around. Freddy served his two years and was released a new creation in Christ.

Freddy continued his walk with God at a Catholic retreat center in Shallowater, Texas called AFM ministries. He went to many retreats and received much emotional healing.

Emotional wounds received by soldiers in battle must be treated just like the physical wounds must be treated. Fighting in wars can cause much inner psychological and emotional wounds and scars that must be treated in order for a soldier to have peace of mind again.

Freddy grew in God and became a lay minister for AFM ministries.

Freddy believed that a spirit of death could become attached to soldiers during their training to kill the enemy.

He believed the spirit of death could also cause soldiers to commit suicide after they were discharged from the military. He believed this spirit needed to be cast out in the name of Jesus.

Freddy gave his life to Jesus and served Jesus the rest of his life. Jesus gave Freddy peace, happiness, a wonderful wife, wonderful children, and wonderful grandchildren.

It was easy to tell from talking to Freddy that he loved his wife, and he loved his children and grandchildren. They were an important part of his life.

**Freddy Rios could truthfully say, "Jesus, I trust in You!"**

**Prayer:** *Heavenly Father, thank You for brave and courageous men like Freddy Rios. He served willingly in an unpopular war. Thank You for his dedication and service to his country. I pray that You give peace of mind and heal the emotional and psychological scars for all the military veterans. In Jesus' name, I pray. Amen!*

Sgt. Freddy Rios

Alfred "Freddy" Rios

# Chapter 5

## Bank Officer

*Therefore,* **if anyone is in Christ, he is a new creation;** *old things have passed away; behold, all things have become new.*
*(2 Corinthians 5:17, NKJV, emphasis added)*

Don is the Founder and Chairman of "Freedom in Jesus Prison Ministries."

Don Castleberry was born in Lubbock, TX in 1939. He is currently 81 years old. Don has four children. He was married to Donna for 37 years. She went to be with the Lord in March 2020. He has one sister who is deceased. Don's mother was a strong believer in Christ. She went to be with the Lord at the age of 52. Don's father was born again at the age of 70, two days before he died.

Don spent six years on his grandparent's farm in Lovington, New Mexico while his mother was sick with tuberculosis. This is where he learned his work ethic. He started driving a tractor at the age of 11. As a child, he loved riding horses and hunting.

At the age of 15, he started drinking and smoking.

He quit high school at the age of 17 and joined the Army. He earned his GED in the Army. Don loved the military and served three years active duty and three years in the National Guard.

Don started working for a finance company in 1963. In 1965, he went to work for a bank. He started out in the banking business by repossessing cars and collecting delinquent accounts. He was promoted to loan officer in 1968 when he was 29 years old. He was a bank loan officer for the next seven years until May 1975. During this time, Don embezzled $300,000 to $400,000. Don did a lot of drinking and partying during this time. He owned a small plane, a 180 Piper Cherokee.

Don turned himself into the FBI in May 1975. The FBI conducted an investigation for 16 months. He was then charged with 21 counts of fraud and embezzlement. However, 19 counts were dropped.

He was charged with two counts of fraud and embezzlement which would carry a six-year sentence.

Don ended up spending four months in Lubbock County jail on weekends and nights. He was paying child support, and the judge wanted him to keep paying the child support. He was allowed to work during the day.

The judge told Don that if he missed one child support payment, he would have to serve the whole six years.

Don was radically saved one weekend while being witnessed to by the Gideon ministry in the county jail. The Gideon's ministry would pass out Bibles and witness to the inmates. This man from the Gideon's ministry was called Noel Williams who was a local dentist.

On January 9, 1977 at 1 PM in the Lubbock County jail, Noel prayed "Father God give Don the "want to" to get saved. The Holy Spirit touched Don at that moment and convicted him of his sin. Don fell to the floor and prayed to receive Jesus into his life. Don was radically saved at that moment, and his life was never the same again.

Don continued to be friends with Noel Williams until his death in 2019 at the age of 88 years. Don conducted his funeral service.

Don became one of five chaplains at the Lubbock County jail that witnessed, passed out Bibles to the prisoners, conducted church services, and taught Bible classes.

Don wanted to learn everything he could about prison ministry. He traveled to Georgia with Johnny Moffitt and the "Worldwide Voice in the Wilderness" prison ministry to preach in a crusade.

Johnny Moffitt encouraged Don to start a prison ministry in Texas which Don did.

Don went to different prisons in Texas conducting services, witnessing, participating in crusades, and helping other prison ministries.

Don started "Freedom in Jesus Prison Ministries" in 1985, and in 1993, the ministry became an official 501c3 nonprofit corporation.

Don became a licensed, ordained minister in 1993 through another prison ministry called "Law of Liberty Ministries."

He started a painting and remodeling business 1986. This business lasted for 22 years until 2008. He financed his ministry through this business. He also gave a lot of jobs to prisoners getting out of jail who needed to work.

Don had his first healing miracle in 1978 when he was feeling sick and went to the doctor who took a lung x-ray which showed a tumor in the left lung. Don and others prayed for healing for this tumor, and 30 days later when he went back for another x-ray, the tumor was gone.

In 1979, Don received the Baptism of the Holy Spirit accompanied by tongues and prayer language. Don said besides being born again, this was the greatest thing that ever happened to him.

The Baptism of the Holy Spirit empowers Christian believers for ministry.

Don married Donna on April 15, 1982. They were married for 37 years. She went to be with the Lord on March 2, 2020. Donna always encouraged Don's prison ministry. Donna also preached at women's prisons. They had a very happy marriage.

There are about 24 out of about 100 prison units in the state of Texas that "Freedom in Jesus Prison Ministries" conducts crusades, preaches, witnesses, conducts church services, and teaches Bible classes.

"Freedom in Jesus Prison Ministries" also has a Correspondence Discipleship Ministry for the prisoners.

There are 25 to 30 volunteers that help with the prison crusades. Crusades are conducted on a Thursday, Friday, Saturday, and Sunday on an average of two times a month.

**Don Castleberry can truly say, "Jesus, I trust in you."**

***Don's Prayer:*** *In the name of Jesus and in the authority of the Word of God and in the power of the Cross, I pray that, Father God, You open the doors to the prisons once again. That the unsaved will have the "want to" to be born again. I pray that You use the Saints that are there to teach new believers the oracles, statutes, and commandments of God that they too may be born again.*

Don, age 20, U.S. Army.

Don, age 51, with daughter, Donna, and grandchildren, Tom and Megan.

Don, age 65, with wife Donna.

Don, age 81, in 2020.

Don in 2020, age 81.

## Chapter 6

## Crash

*Who may worship in your sanctuary, Lord? Who may enter your presence on your holy hill?* **Those who lead blameless lives and do what is right, speaking the truth from sincere hearts. Those who refuse to gossip or harm their neighbors or speak evil of their friends.**
*(Psalm 15:1-3, NLT, emphasis added)*

Le Roy Duran was having a nice day playing golf with friends at the Reese Air Force base golf course in Lubbock, Texas on July 13, 2007. He finished his golf game and was headed back to his home in Abernathy, Texas at sunset.

Le Roy was driving on Interstate 27 when he fell asleep at the wheel and crashed into a guard rail near New Deal, Texas. His life was changed in an instant of time. In the mere blink of an eye, his life would never be the same. He was wearing his seatbelt when the driver's door was ripped off and he was ejected 120 feet, ripping off both arms at the shoulder. Le Roy has undergone 19 surgeries since then related to his car accident.

He survived only by a series of miracles and the power of God.

Through this whole ordeal, Le Roy learned patience and endurance in all things.

However, let's go back to the beginning. Le Roy was born in Abernathy, Texas on October 7, 1961. He has one brother and four sisters. His mother worked for Texas Tech University 31 years before retiring. His father was a John Deere tractor mechanic for 35 years. His father had nine brothers and two sisters. His Mom had four sisters and six brothers.

Le Roy and his family lived in the country until 1970 when his family moved into Abernathy, Texas. In 1969, Leroy noticed his father and brother would leave home in the morning before sunrise while it was still dark and come back in the evening at sundown.

They worked all day driving a tractor on farms.

Le Roy said a prayer that day asking God if they could move into town. He thought his father and brother were having to work too hard.

The next year in 1970, God answered his prayer. His family moved into Abernathy and his father got a job as a mechanic.

Le Roy did not have a good relationship with his father. Even though he received much attention and was a little spoiled by his paternal grandparents. As a child, Le Roy used to think, "Why can't I have a good father like the good fathers on I see on TV." At the age of 13, Le Roy started using alcohol and marijuana to numb the emotional pain from the poor relationship he had with his father.

Le Roy also got into a lot of fights in high school because of racism between Whites and Hispanics. He graduated from Abernathy High School in 1979.

Le Roy wanted to get away from small-town life, so he joined the U.S. Army in December 1979. He shipped out to Fort Knox, Kentucky the day after Christmas on December 26, 1979.

There was three feet of snow at Fort Knox when he arrived. He went to tank school and was sent to Germany for two years. He became a Captain's driver.

Le Roy did very well in the military and became an E4 after only 2 ½ years. He was discharged from the Army after three years and moved back to Lubbock, Texas.

He married Sandra in 1983 and had two daughters.

The marriage lasted five years and ended in divorce in 1988. Le Roy said, "I didn't know how to act as a father and husband. I didn't have any good role models." His ex-wife, Sandra, asked him not to have any contact with his girls. Le Roy agreed and did not see his girls for 10 years. Le Roy said, "Not seeing my girls for 10 years was the biggest mistake I ever made in my entire life."

In his own words, Le Roy describes his journey with his two daughters:

### *Le Roy's Journey With His Daughters*

*Jennifer Ann Duran Hearon DOB. 8/8/84 (age 36) Hale Center, Tx.*
*Valerie Michele Duran 2/20/86 (age 34) Santa Rosa, N.M.*

*Sandra and I were both young adults which were still exploring life, as well as developing our identities, and with little or no idea on how we were to succeed in life as adults, or as parents.*

*We can play the blame game, but the reality was that we both had no clue on how to apply God's principles into our lives. Our marriage came with partying, friends and social events which provided the both of us opportunities to sin, not realizing the consequences?*

*We both came from your typical Hispanic Catholic families, where both our parents worked long hard hours, with little to show for their efforts. American Hispanic History reveals that there were little to no education or employment opportunities through the 60's-mid 70's (when our parents were young adults). Our parents for whatever reason, did not get the family development support from their parents or the church, so it's fair to say, neither did we.*

*After five years of marriage (both of us being in our mid 20's,) Sandra filed for divorce and on the way out of the courthouse, she asked me to stay away from her daughters and if I agreed, she would not ask for any child support. While at that very moment I was still processing the life event which just changed our lives (pride and anger occupied my senses), and not to overlook the events which led to this day, I responded with a stern sure!*

*Additionally, my agreement was supported by the recent courtroom experience where Sandra's attorney played hardball with me in the courtroom. While I was representing myself (thank God the lady Judge had the decency to tell the attorney to chill out, and lets just work through the process), to support my not being in agreement with a divorce.*

*Additionally, during our separation period prior to the divorce, while I was living in Albuquerque, we would meet in Santa Rosa, New Mexico (at a highway rest area for travelers) to transfer the children (daughters were 2.5-3.5 years old) from one parent to the other, after our daughters spent three days with me.*

*On one particular transfer where it was time for the girls to go back with their mother, a female friend of mine took the girls to the restroom and on the way back to the car Jennifer regurgitated from stress/nerves. In my opinion, Jennifer understood the transfer of the girls from one parent to the other was about to happen, and watching her regurgitate, broke my heart into a million pieces.*

*My mind went straight back in time to my Junior High School days, when I would spend the weekend with a couple of friends of mine whose parents were divorced. Their parents would talk ugly about the other parent (in our presence), and this would cause my friends to cry from confusion, pain, and shame. I did not wish for our girls to go down* the same path as I experienced with my friends, so this also weighed into my answer when I was asked to stay away.

Upon my return to West Texas, I made contact with my oldest daughter Jennifer, through a couple of teachers (I met at church-God connects people-to help people) who worked at the High School she attended. I still understood that when her mother found out, that bridge would need to be crossed. My daughters also happened to be friends with a boy in High School, who was the son of old friends of ours and this was another contact source.

Towards the end of 2000, I found myself facing the opportunity of my lifetime, meeting my daughter. Jennifer and I met a couple of times, which allowed me to share how much I have missed and loved both she and her sister. I was able to give her pictures of their childhood, which I held onto, and Valerie, my other daughter was not at the point to where she wanted to meet me.

After our second meeting, later that day, I found myself looking outside the kitchen window, thinking of what I could do or things I could buy to help Jennifer love me. I was immediately checked by the Holy Spirit. The Holy Spirit told me that the things I could do or things I could buy Jennifer, would only develop material love (fake conditional love) from Jennifer. The Holy Spirit went on to tell me who I thought cared for my daughters in my absence, my *response was the Lord took care of our daughters. He said, "Correct, and do you think that I'm just going to step aside an allow you to take over simply because you retuned home, no!"*

*He said, "How much time would you like to spend with your daughters? The short amount of time that we all have to live on earth or for eternity in My Kingdom?" I said, "Duh! Eternity in Your Kingdom Father." He then said, "You continue on your journey with the church, daily learning how to die to yourself and the world, and I will continue to care for your daughters."*

*From that moment forward, in the Spirit, I released my daughters lives unto the Lord, and have focused on consecrating every moment of my life unto the Lords Will for my life. The Holy Spirit then brought into my remembrance, my experience at the church in Austin, Tx. with "The Katina's" and their song "On the Other Side."*

*Not long after our second meeting, I noticed Jennifer giving me the cold shoulder, then she was not answering or returning my calls. I would locate her place of employment and drop by, but after the second time I could tell she was uncomfortable, so I shared with her that I will always love you and that I would prove it to her by staying away.*

*Here comes the bridge which needs to be crossed. I was told by mutual friends of ours, that Jennifer's mother did not like the fact that we have met, in addition to Jennifer having photo's which I gave her. I knew that I broke our verbal agreement about staying away from our girls, and that I needed to prepare for either a call or court summons from her mother, it was the court summons.*

*The Court summons requested that I report to the State Child Support Division, and that attorneys were not necessary as this was a preliminary setting to see if we could settle this without having to use the court system.*

*I spent time, a lot of time, with the Lord prior to the court date. The amount of thoughts, memories, good bad or indifferent, which went through my head, day and night were overwhelming. I wanted revenge, I wanted to have access to my daughters, but at the same time, the Lord hit me about my new journey with Him, the church and His Will for my life. How can I represent the Lord with an unforgiving heart?*

*The Holy Spirit reminded me of the last years of our marriage, separation, and divorce court, they were all filled with deceit, anger, blame and power plays. "Son," I heard the Lord say, "I need you to not handle this as a person of the world, I need you to handle it as my son. We are to love, forgive, and help others at all times, and I need you to show an act of kindness and agree with whatever the mother of your children ask for."*

The day of court, I arrived in Peace. I entered the building, then the appointed room to introduce myself and the court appointed Legal Aid representative, acknowledged all who were present, Sandra, myself and Legal Aid. The Legal Aid rep. spent awhile with Sandra; she then made her way to me. She again introduced herself, the position and capacity of her appointment, and then asked if I had any questions for her before she introduced Sandra's request.

Sandra was asking for 100% of Child Support back pay, plus, medical insurance. The 100% C.S. backpay amounted to $105,000.00 and the medical insurance was around $100.00 per month. I told the Legal Aid Rep. that I accepted the amounts which Sandra was asking for. Immediately, the Legal Aid Rep. stated that I didn't have to agree and that I could dispute the Back-pay amount and it would be reduced to $52,500.00. I told the Legal Aid Rep. that I appreciated her sharing the information with me, but that I had given my word to the Lord, that I would honor what the mother of our children asked for.

From 2002-2007, monthly, I paid $400-$600 Child Support. After my auto accident, and six-month hospital stay, I was not able to pay, because I was not working. However, once I was released from the hospital and I qualified for Social Security Disability, Sandra took me back to Child Support

Court for the original monthly amount of $600, she was awarded $300 per month.

For the next 11 years beginning sometime in 2008, the Child Support payment of $300, was automatically deducted from my monthly SSI-Disb. Check, in addition, the remaining  balanced I owed accumulated interest like a consumer loan does (shocker), so I paid extra against the accumulating interest (shocker)?

This went on for roughly 11 years. In 2019 my principle and interest combined balances=$40k. Sandra's husband and I discussed the possibility of a settlement payoff of $20k cash (the Lord's Favor). I applied for a Reverse Mortgage Loan from my credit union, and everything went well until closing. My home is paid off; however, the credit unions title department was not accepting a title document from my attorney's office, and after 2 months of haggling over the document issue, I pulled the plug on the loan app.

I leaned into the Lord, as it was, He who closed the door on the Reverse Mortgage Loan, so I asked Him, "What do I do now," He said, "Have faith and trust in Me." As with all things in my life since the accident, I have learned to die physically and to the ways of the world, and I have learned to lean unto the Lord for all my needs. The Lord basically had a friend, who is a brother in Christ pay the $20k cash which settled my Child Support Case!

*Since the year 2000, I've met with Jennifer and Valerie twice, and for whatever reason, we have not been able to develop a relationship (if you ask the Lord for Wisdom on my situation, I'm certain He will).*

*Through this 17-year struggle of paying money, and not having any interaction with my daughters has had many a people (relatives-friends) call me out. They could not understand how the courts could have me pay while the girls are adults, they don't visit with me, and their mother is married, and they have 2 incomes (what a deal).*

*Still, I have been at peace due to my past conversation with the Lord, when He asked me how much time would I like to spend with my daughters? The short amount of time that we all have to live on earth or for eternity in My Kingdom? I accepted Eternity in His Kingdom. He then said that I was to continue on my journey with the church, daily learning how to die to myself and the world, and that He will continue to care for my daughters.*

*Understanding that God has given me opportunities to right the wrongs of my past (in respect to my being a husband and father), plus be with Him and my daughters in His Kingdom for eternity, is mind blowing! Heaven will be filled with love and peace, with no memories of the past, however, we will know one another. Additionally, He asked me to not fight the Child Support Case as a person of the world would (defend yourself and fight for what is best for you). He asked me to show an act of kindness and agree with whatever Sandra asked for.*

*The Lord was asking me to have the same heart when paying the monthly Child Support money, as I do when I give my monthly Tithe to Him. For whatever reason the Lord did not allow the Reverse Mortgage Loan to go through and after much prayer, He had a brother in Christ bless me with $20k to settle and payoff my Child Support Case (only God)!*

*I pray that throughout my life, you have been able to see the Lord tear me down, piece by piece, to where I could not even dress or feed myself. Yet, He has given me the ability to pay off a $105k debt., and have nothing to show for it (from the worlds view). Yet, every month for 17 years I had PEACE, knowing that I was working towards a righteous goal of living life with His daughters in Heaven for ETERNITY!*

*Father, thank you for caring, providing, and protecting my daughters in my absence.*

*Thank you for developing Jennifer into a special sister, lady, wife and mother. Father, I pray that you protect her as she cares for others in the hospital, renew her strength daily, so that she may be able to fulfill her nursing, and family responsibilities.*

*Father, I lift up Valerie to you, I pray that she can see the value which you have placed within her. Father, I thank you for also developing Valerie into a special sister, lady, and mother. Father, I pray for her continued development and that she will continue to help others in need. Father, I pray the blood of Jesus over her, protect her from evil, and restore her daily, so that she can allow you to work through her, while helping others.*

*The Lord's servant!*

*Amen!*

During his separation and divorce, Le Roy moved to Albuquerque, New Mexico for about six years and became an electrician. He enjoyed the single life in Albuquerque. Then he moved to Austin, Texas. His brother ran the finances for a few health clubs in Austin. Le Roy worked with his brother for about three years learning about finances. He worked a few years for a mortgage company and a few more years for Dell Computer.

During this time, he was invited to church by the best-looking girl at his work site. Her name was Maria.

Le Roy said on a scale of 1 to 10 with 10 being the highest, she rated a 13. So of course, he said "yes."

He started attending the World of Pentecost Church in Austin, Texas with Maria. About 3,000 people attended this church. A gospel music group called "The Katinas" from Hawaii was performing one evening at his church.

They sang one song called "On the Other Side" that really touched Le Roy. After church, he told them how much that song meant to him. He told them how much his heart ached to see his daughters, and how he hoped to see his daughters "on the other side" in heaven.

The singers were touched by his story and all of them gathered around him and laid hands on him and prayed for the restoration of the relationship with his daughters.

One day in April 1999, Le Roy had gone to church with Maria as usual. This would be a day like no other. This was the day that he would have his salvation experience. This was the day he would have his born-again conversion experience.

Right after the praise and worship team had finished, and the preacher had just started his sermon, Le Roy started feeling really hot.

He turned to Maria and said, "I am really hot. Is the air-conditioner working?"

She said, "Yes."

Le Roy then said to Maria, "It feels like I got a fishhook in my chest pulling me to the front altar." (Jesus really is a fisher of men.)

Maria said, "Do what you got to do."

Le Roy stood up and walked down to the pulpit while the preacher was preaching.

While he was walking up to the altar, he started sweating, crying, and shaking uncontrollably. The Holy Spirit was all over him. Leroy felt like he was being purged of all his past sins.

When he arrived at the front of the church, an associate pastor met him and said, "Do you believe that Jesus Christ died for your sins and that he rose again on the third day?"

Leroy said, "Yes!"

The associate pastor told Le Roy that the Holy Spirit wanted to tell him, "Your sins have been forgiven, and the curse has been broken and you will inherit the riches of your forefathers."

Le Roy felt that the curse that was broken was alcoholism, and that "the riches of his forefathers" meant eternal peace with where he is and what he is doing.

In May 1999, Le Roy started having godly dreams. He could only fall asleep while listening to gospel music.

In October 1999, he was having dreams of his mother getting sick. His mother had two open-heart surgeries, 13 years apart. Le Roy called his mother and asked her if she was getting sick. She said, yes, she was getting sick again.

In a dream, God told Le Roy to move back to Abernathy to take care of his parents.

Le Roy said to God, "Hell no!" There is no way I can live with my dad. Besides that, I have a great job! I have a great church! And I live in a great city! And you want me to give all that up!"

God responded in a later dream and said, "You can always get a great job! You can always live in a great city! You can always go to a great church! But you are only going to have one set of parents! I am just asking you to do for them what they did for you when you were little!"

God was giving Le Roy the opportunity to honor the 5th Commandment "Honor your father and mother" when God gave him the opportunity to move back with his parents.

In December 1999, Le Roy went to a Christmas party in Austin, Texas on the roof of a high-rise building. He left his friends and walked to the edge of the building and looking at the moon he said, "God I can't live like this anymore, partying and womanizing, I will live for you under one condition, that I don't have to be a fake Christian."

In June 2000, Leroy resigned his job and gave two weeks' notice to his employer. He gave away all of his furniture.

While driving back to Abernathy, he prayed to God for a sign that he was doing the right thing. He turned on the radio and the song came on "On the Other Side." This song confirmed to him that this was God's will for him.

Le Roy moved back in with his parents in Abernathy, TX to take care of them, but he still did not have a good relationship with his dad. The first four years back with his mom and dad were normal. His dad would take her to her medical appointments. Le Roy worked during the day in Lubbock at Singular Wireless.

Le Roy would watch TV with his mom in the evening. They liked to watch the Reba McEntire show and the George Lopez show.

Le Roy wanted to find a good church to go to in Lubbock, TX. He had been praying about this. One day, he was going down 82$^{nd}$ St. in Lubbock driving east when he came to the intersection of 82$^{nd}$ and Slide. He sensed the Holy Spirit was telling him to turn right on Slide St. Le Roy turned right and went down Slide Street until he felt an impression on his chest when he drove by Church on the Rock.

Le Roy knew that God was telling him this was the church for him. He attended this church for seven years from 2000 to 2007.

The Church on the Rock was a small church at this time. Le Roy sensed that the Holy Spirit was telling him that this was a small church that would grow into a large Noah's Ark. He loved the praise and worship service. He attended the first transformation class that helps people transform into Christian life.

Le Roy wanted his pride to die, so he decided to go to the altar every time there was an altar call. This went on for three months and Pastor Jackie White noticed he was coming up to the altar every time.

He asked Le Roy his name and told him the Holy Spirit said, "The curses have been broken and you will inherit the riches of your forefathers." These were the same words that were spoken to him by the associate pastor at the church in Austin. Le Roy felt like this was God's confirmation that he was in the right church.

Le Roy made some friends at this church that would later prove to be a godsend during his recovery from his accident.

He met Associate Pastor Delay who mentored him in his Christian walk. The Lord used Associate Pastor Delay to develop Le Roy for future pastoral responsibilities.

Le Roy met a godly man at the men's ministry meeting called Fred Watson. Fred was a spiritual father to Le Roy. Le Roy felt like Fred Watson's countenance was like an angel.

Le Roy met Rebecca Watson at church who was the wife of Fred Watson. In June 2007, she had gone to the rear parking lot after church and the Holy Spirit told her to go back and pray for Le Roy. She went back in church and Le Roy was setting in the front row to the right of the pulpit.

She asked Le Roy for his permission to pray for him, and Le Roy agreed. She sensed the Holy Spirit was saying to get the anointing oil from the altar and pour it over him which she did. One month later on July 13, 2007, Le Roy had his car accident.

Le Roy met Vanessa Parker and John Thurston at church. Vanessa was a nurse at Covenant Medical Center. Le Roy, Vanessa, and John were in the first session of the two-year "Ministry Training School."

They became like brothers and sisters. Le Roy and John also went on three mission trips together. They developed a tight bond that would be needed later for Le Roy's recovery.

Ironically, through Gods eyes, he put together a family of friends from three genetically different backgrounds. Vanessa is black, John is white, and Le Roy is Hispanic. They became spiritual siblings and did everything possible to help Le Roy throughout his six-month journey.

Vanessa kept his immediate family and church family updated 1-3 times daily with emails about his medical status along with pending medical procedures and results. Her 20+ years nursing experience plus being spiritually adopted into Le Roy's family and having access to him, gave his family peace. Having access and knowing when blood was being transfused the first two days was paramount in having people pray over the transfusions.

Vanessa also arranged for finances for food, utilities, and travel for Le Roy's parents and siblings while traveling. She took on this responsibility from day one throughout the full six months.

His mom's health started deteriorating in 2005. Le Roy was so engrossed in his career and Christian development that he really did not know how much his mother's health was declining. His mom's health got even worse in 2006, and he and his dad took 12 hour shifts in caring for her. One sister came to help them.

One week prior to his car accident his mom was given three days to live due to her heart failure. She prayed to see her son back home, and she lived another eight months. Le Roy was in the hospital and rehab six of those months.

Le Roy went golfing at the Reese Air Force Base golf course in Lubbock, Texas on July 13, 2007. After his golf game, he headed back home. At sunset, he was driving back to Abernathy, TX on Interstate 27. He fell asleep at the wheel near New Deal, Texas, and he hit a guardrail.

There was an off-duty police officer driving behind Le Roy when he hit the guardrail.

Le Roy does not remember much about the accident, but the off-duty police officer was a witness to the whole event and later told Le Roy exactly what happened.

Le Roy was wearing his seatbelt when the accident happened. Leroy hit the guardrail, and the driver's door was ripped off.

The seatbelt severed both arms at the shoulders, and he was ejected 120 feet from the car.

He had a road rash from the head to the toe on the left side. He lost 7 pints of his blood at the accident site. His body type holds 9 to 10 pints of blood. The off-duty police officer quickly radioed for a life-flight helicopter. The emergency medical crew arrived quickly and started transfusing blood to him.

They also performed an emergency tracheostomy at the crash site. Le Roy flatlined twice at the crash site and was revived.

Le Roy says he only opened his eyes twice at the crash site, once while he was laying on the ground and once when the tracheostomy procedure was being performed.

He was flown to Covenant Medical Center in Lubbock, TX. He had six surgeries the first week and flatlined four more times.

He was in incredible pain.

He was put into an induced coma on a ventilator for two months because he was in so much pain.

After Le Roy arrived in the emergency room, there was a discussion amongst the doctors about whether to try and reattach the arms or not. Three doctors did not see any sense in trying to reattach both arms. However, there was one trauma surgeon on call that day that wanted to reattach the arms.

He was a believer in the Lord. Artificial shoulder joints and elbow joints were made, and the arms were reattached.

Le Roy talked to this doctor three or four months later, and the doctor was impressed with his progress.

Le Roy was in the hospital and rehab for a total of six months.

His friend, John Thurston, was living in Colorado Springs, Colorado during this time but still visited him every other weekend. John noticed how much pain Le Roy was in and asked the doctor if there was anything else, he could do.

At one point, Le Roy had given up on learning to walk again. John yelled at him and told him to go out in the hall and start walking.

And Le Roy did just that. He made it to the hallway and started walking.

Le Roy completed his rehabilitation and went home in December 2007. His mother went to be with the Lord two months later.

The total cost for his hospital and rehabilitation was $1.8 million. The Insurance paid 80%, but he was responsible for the 20% co-pay. The 20% co-pay came to $610,000. Anette Taylor, also from his church, worked at the hospital and asked him to apply for the "forgiveness program."

Le Roy applied for it and received it. He has a zero balance. Praise the Lord!

He still has problems with chronic pain in the hands and forearms. But he is able to drive a car and operate a cell phone.

Once after rehab, he had an out of body experience. Two ladies and Pastor Delay were praying for him, and the room turned red and about six demons popped out of thin air.

There was one snake demon on his right bedrail about 6 inches in diameter. Le Roy said, "You are not going to get me." Then he passed out, and when he awoke, the demons were gone.

This bothered him, and he asked the Lord about it. He became fearful about going to hell. The Lord came to him in a dream and said, "You are not going to hell. I just wanted to show you that hell is real. Most people that have out of body experiences share celestial things about Heaven and Angels."

Le Roy volunteers with "Freedom in Jesus Prison Ministries" and "Jubilee Prison Ministry." He is also a volunteer chaplain assistant with the Texas Department of Corrections and Justice. He teaches Bible classes at the prison unit in Plainview, Texas.


**Le Roy Duran can truly say, "Jesus, I trust in you."**

*Prayer:* *Heavenly Father, I pray for healing for those with chronic pain. I pray for restoration of relationships between fathers and children. Thank You for your miracle working power. Thank you for all the miracles that you performed so that Le Roy can be full of life today and ministering the Word of God to others. In Jesus' name, I pray. Amen!*

Le Roy Duran in 2006.

Le Roy, age 58, in 2020.

Le Roy Duran in 2003.

Le Roy in the Army in 1980 at Fort Knox, Kentucky.

Le Roy in the hospital after accident in 2007.

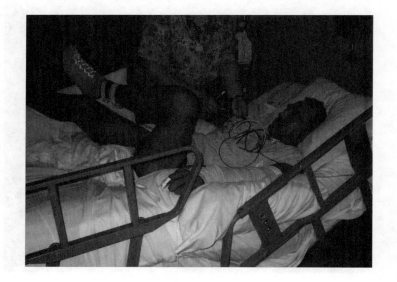

John, Le Roy, and Vanessa in December 2007.

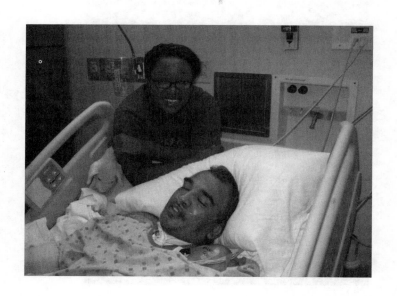

Le Roy and Vanessa after the accident in 2007.

Le Roy in Rehab in 2007.

Le Roy with the policeman and his wife who were behind Le Roy when the accident occurred. Photo was taken in October 2007.

Le Roy and his daughters, Jennifer and Valerie in 1986.

Le Roy and his daughter, Valerie, in 2016.

Le Roy and his daughter,
Jennifer, in 2000.

## Chapter 7

## Football Star

*He who dwells in the secret place of the Most High shall abide under the shadow of the Almighty.* ***I will say of the Lord, "He is my refuge and my fortress; my God, in Him I will trust."***
*(Psalm 91:1, NKJV, emphasis added)*

Brian Thompson was an African American football star in high school. In 11th grade, he landed a five-year football scholarship to the University of Miami. But he made a bad decision and went to prison in his senior year of high school, two months before he was to graduate.

Brian was born in Houston, Texas on September 17, 1971, and he lived most of his life there. He has no siblings. His father was a pastor but was never involved in his life.

His mom was addicted to drugs during his childhood. Brian was raised by his great-grandmother who took him to church every Sunday. He describes himself as a loner in school. He skipped school a lot in the 6th and 7th grade and started drinking beer and smoking marijuana. In the eighth grade, the school told him he could play sports if he kept his grades up.

He weighed 171 pounds in the eighth grade and became a running back on the football team. He ran an 80-yard touchdown for his eighth-grade football team. He became very popular with the girls.

He had several high schools trying to recruit him to come play football at their school. He chose the high school that was closest to his home which was the Phyllis Wheatley High School.

He started playing for the varsity high school team when he was a freshman. His freshman, sophomore, and junior year in high school went very well for him. He became very popular in high school because he was a great running back on the football team. In his best football game, he had 10 carries, running for 171 yards, and scored three touchdowns.

In 11th grade, he was offered a five-year football scholarship at the University of Miami after he graduated high school.

In his senior year of high school, he moved out of his grandmother's house and moved in with a friend. He made a bad decision that changed his life. He decided to start selling drugs to make money to take to college with him. One night his friend was playing with a gun and shot himself. An ambulance was called, and he was taken to the emergency room.

The next morning his house was raided by the Drug Task Force. They seized $1,400 worth of cocaine. In March 1990, two months before he was to graduate high school, he received a 10-year prison sentence for drug possession. He went to Central Unit Prison in Sugarland, Texas and served 11 months and 27 days.

After his release from prison, he went back to his old neighborhood. He had no job skills. He started drinking heavily. He started selling drugs again to survive. He ran into a girl he used to go to school with. She invited him to her house, and Brian got into an argument with the guy she had been hanging out with. Brian grabbed her gun to shoot the other guy and accidentally shot her. He had only been out of prison for 90 days, and now, he was going back to prison a 2nd time for 10 years.

He went to a prison in Gatesville, Texas and served the whole 10 years. His mother started writing to him. She had gone to prison and gave her life over to Jesus Christ. She was out of prison and going to church, and she and others had started praying for Brian. His mother started sending him Christian materials and he read them. Brian was starting to have more and more thoughts of church, thoughts of Jesus, and thoughts of getting saved and giving his life over to the Lord.

There was one guy that he and a friend had been fighting with in prison. Brian decided he was going to stab this guy one morning, but the guy went to church that morning. Brian decided to go to church to get this guy. It was a large church service of 350 people. However, the Holy Spirit started dealing with Brian.

Brian told God, "If you will call me out, then I will believe."

The preacher started walking down the aisle and said, "I am looking for a dude with teardrops."

Brian had a tattoo teardrop on his face. The preacher stopped where Brian was sitting in his seat and looked at his teardrop tattoo and called him out.

The preacher said to him, "Are you ready to receive what the Lord has for you?"

Brian said yes and received Christ that day. Brian started reading the Bible and understood it through God's help. He started growing spiritually. Brian was eight years into his 10-year prison sentence, and he finished his last two years as a Christian.

Brian was released from prison when he finished his 10-year sentence.

However, he made the mistake of going back to his old neighborhood with no work skills. He felt a lot of pressure to get a job. He found a job, but he started drinking and womanizing again. He started missing a lot of days of work and was fired.

Desperate for money, he started snatching moneybags from people going to and from banks. He stayed out of prison 18 months. Then he was arrested for robbery and was sentenced to 14 years. He served nine of those years and was paroled.

This was his third time in prison. He was tired of being away from his family. He started getting serious about God, and he fully surrendered to the will of God this time.

He started teaching Bible studies in prison. He started preaching at prison church services.

He wanted to be led by the Holy Spirit, and he began to learn the voice of the Holy Spirit.

He was paroled after nine years.

He was released in May 2013. This was his last trip to prison. He had gone to prison three times and served a total of 20 years in prison.

After his release, he went to Lindale, Texas and enrolled at Calvary Commission. He met his wife, Brittanya, there the first year. They were married in 2014.

Brian went back to Houston for six months. His family did not like him being married to a white woman, so they moved to Abilene, Texas. The parole board released him from his leg monitor after one year.

He left Abilene, TX and moved to Gatesville Texas in 2015. He stayed in Gatesville for one year. He had a construction job, but he was struggling financially. He started drinking again and was at the point of splitting up with his wife. His wife called Stephen Canup who was involved with the "Freedom in Jesus Prison Ministries" for counseling.

Brian and Brittanya moved to Levelland, TX in 2016. Stephen Canup help them find a place to live. Brian and Brittanya started going to Transformation Church which made a huge difference in their life. They started going to transformation classes and were discipled by the church. They started doing prison ministry together through "Freedom in Jesus Prison Ministries."

Brittanya went back to school and got her cosmetology license.

Brian got his Class A Commercial Driver's License.

At first, Brian had a hard time finding a job. When employers found out he had been in prison, they did not want him. His bills were starting to stack up, and he needed money. Brian sensed the Holy Spirit was telling him to say "thank you" instead of getting mad at the employers. So that is what he started doing.

Brian was learning to listen to the Holy Spirit and be led by Jesus. One day, the Holy Spirit said to Brian, "Call 84 Lumber." Brian called them, and they offered him a job and asked him to start that day.

In 2017, Brian went to the hospital to get blood pressure medication. His troponin level was high, and they said he had a heart attack. He was sent to the Heart Hospital in Lubbock, Texas. The cardiologist wanted to do an angiogram the next morning. The Holy Spirit said to Brian, "Start worshiping God." His wife stayed with him that night, and they both worshiped God during the night. The doctor ran the angiogram that morning, and it showed no blockage. The doctor released him.

Brian was healed due to his obedience to the Holy Spirit.

Things have gone well for Brian and Brittanya the last four years in Levelland, Texas. Brian currently drives a truck for a concrete company.

During the last four years, a ministry friend felt God was leading her to give $4,500 to Brian, and she did.

Another ministry friend felt like God was leading her to give him a truck, and she did.

Brian has learned to discern the voice of God and to obey the voice of God.

**Brian can truly say, "Jesus, I trust in you."**

**Prayer:** *Heavenly Father, I pray that you touch the heart of each person reading this book. Help them to discern the voice of God and to obey the voice of God. Thank You, God, for giving us the example of Brian in discerning and following the will of God. In Jesus' name, I pray. Amen!*

Brian in 2010 in the Eastham Prison
Unit in Texas.

Brian and Brittanya in 2018.

Brian and Brittanya in 2017.

# Chapter 8

# Park Avenue

*For though we live in the world, we do not wage war as the world does. The weapons we fight with are not the weapons of the world. On the contrary, they have divine power to demolish strongholds. We demolish arguments and every pretension that sets itself up against the knowledge of God,* **and we take captive every thought to make it obedient to Christ.**
*(2 Corinthians 10:3-5, NIV, emphasis added)*

Stephen Canup is currently the President of "Freedom in Jesus Prison Ministries." He has written and published three books. Stephen was born on April 20, 1952 and is currently 68 years old.

He was once a certified public accountant (CPA) employed by the world's largest accounting firm on Park Avenue in New York City. He went from Park Avenue to being homeless and eventually to prison. Stephen went from a six-figure income to being penniless and sleeping on park benches and stairwell landings in parking garages.

Stephen was born at Ft. Benning, GA. His father spent 20 years in the Army then retired. He has two older brothers and one younger sister. He also has an adopted son. Stephen's family moved to Lubbock, TX when he was eight years old.

As a boy, he went to Highland Baptist Church in Lubbock, TX. He even made a profession of faith and was baptized when he was twelve years old. He always called himself a Christian, but he was just deceiving himself. Stephen actually became a born-again Christian while in prison on April 20, 2009. At that point he confessed his sins and repented of them. He asked Jesus to be the Lord and Savior of his life, and he has lived his life for Christ since that time.

Stephen graduated with honors from Coronado High School in 1970. He then entered Texas Tech University and graduated in 1974 with a Bachelor of Business Administration (BBA) degree in accounting.

He worked for a couple of accounting firms and ended up employed by KPMG Peat Marwick which was the world's largest accounting firm. He became a partner at 29 years old.

In 1987, Stephen was 35 years old, and he had achieved the American dream. He was making over $200,000 annual income working as a CPA on Park Avenue on the 27th floor of a high-rise building in New York City.

He was living in Darien, Connecticut, and he would take a commuter train to Grand Central Station in New York City, then walk to his office building. Stephen Canup was a partner with the world's largest accounting firm. He had a wonderful Christian wife and a healthy son. His automobiles were paid off, his credit record was spotless, and he was having a custom home built. He had over $100,000 in available credit on his credit cards. Outwardly, he was on top of the world and appeared very successful. Inwardly, he was restless, empty, lost, and confused. He was addicted to success, money, and pride.

Stephen was not thankful or grateful to God for his success. He did not desire God in his life. Stephen stated, "My conceit, greed, impatience, pride, and selfishness were about to destroy my life."

Two years later in 1989 he transferred to Dallas, TX. Then he made the worst decision of his life which started a 20-year downward spiral and ended with him penniless, sleeping on a park bench, then to prison.

Stephen decided to quit his job, leave his wife and son, and go to Nashville to pursue fame and riches in the music business. He lost it all within a year. He filed for bankruptcy. For the first time in his life, he felt like a failure. He became addicted to crack cocaine, marijuana, alcohol, sex, pornography, and gambling. During this time, he participated in almost every form of sexual immorality and perversion.

He felt empty inside for years and nothing could fill the void in his soul. He felt hopeless and pushed away every friend and family member. This life-style left Stephen so empty and depressed that he attempted several failed suicide attempts.

From 2002 to 2005, Stephen was unemployed. He stayed with one friend rent-free for three years. This friendship ended when he started using marijuana, again. Stephen then found a job and an apartment. By 2006, he was fired from his job and became homeless. For the next year and a half, he lived in a tent on a wooded hillside in South Nashville.

He often slept on a park bench or in building stairwells. He was addicted to alcohol, pornography, and crack cocaine. During a five-day binge on drugs and alcohol, and going most of that time without any sleep, Stephen made more bad decisions. Stephen was arrested for "solicitation of a minor."

Stephen ended up with three charges that brought a total sentence of six years. He violated the terms of his probation and was sent to a medium-security prison in Nashville to serve out his sentence.

In prison, Stephen felt life was hopeless. He felt like life was over. He began to realize his need for God. He asked the prison chaplain for a Bible to read. The chaplain gave him a Gideon New Testament. For the next 10 months, he would read the Bible a few minutes each night before bed, but he did not attend church services.

By April 2009, Stephen was ready to give his life fully over to Jesus. On April 20, 2009, which was Stephen's 57th birthday, Jesus became not only his Savior but his Lord. Stephen confessed his sins and repented and asked Jesus to take over his life. Stephen was rebaptized in prison. Stephen felt like his burden of guilt, shame, and remorse was lifted. Even though he was in prison, he felt free.

The next 22 months passed quickly. He served a total of 32 months in prison beginning at the age of 56.

He wrote letters to his two older brothers and his younger sister and his son to ask for their forgiveness. His two older brothers forgave him while he was still in prison. His sister forgave him after he was released from prison. His son forgave him two years after he was released from prison.

Stephen believes the secret to stay free from addictions and resist temptations is to submit to God.

Stephen was on the Registry of Sex Offenders from 2010 to 2020. Jesus changed Stephen from the inside out. He is a new creation in Christ. There is always hope, even for a sex offender. Jesus can and does forgive any sin that a person will confess to Him.

Stephen is now President of "Freedom in Jesus Prison Ministries." He preaches and conducts Bible studies in prisons and at other places.

**Stephen Canup can truly say, "Jesus, I trust in you."**

***Stephen's Prayer:*** *I pray that You fill me with the knowledge of your will through all spiritual wisdom and understanding. I pray this in order that I may live a life worthy of the Lord Jesus and please Him in every way: bearing fruit in every good work, growing in the knowledge of you, God, so that I may be strengthened with all power according to Your glorious might so that I may have great endurance and patience and joyfully give You thanks. Amen.*

Stephen Canup in March 2015.

Cassidy, Don, Albert, Stephen

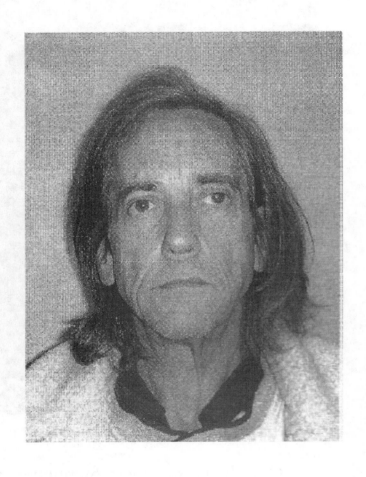

Stephen in November 2007 before he
came to Christ.

Stephen after he came to Christ.

## Chapter 9

## Meth Addiction

*"And whenever you stand praying, if you have anything against anyone, forgive him, that your Father in heaven may also forgive you your trespasses. But if you do not forgive, neither will your Father in heaven forgive your trespasses."*
*(Mark 11:25-26, NKJV, emphasis added)*


Jennifer Fortenberry was a meth addict for 18 years, and she was in prison three times. The meth addiction caused her to have mental illness with symptoms of drug-induced schizophrenia. She was depressed, paranoid, hearing voices, and seeing hallucinations. After she was released from prison the third time, Jennifer was tested for employment and they told her that she would never be able to hold job. They told her to apply to the government for a mental disability.

However, Jennifer turned to God and his awesome power. God delivered her from her mental illness and all of its symptoms, and God delivered her from meth addiction.

God told Jennifer to start applying for jobs and go to work. God told her not to worry, she could do this. Jennifer listened to God and was hired at the first job she applied for which was a telephone marketing services company.

After one month, Jennifer earned the "Employee of the Month" award. After nine months, she received a better job offer at "Wholesale Payments." Jennifer has been with this employer for six years. She earned the "Telemarketer of the Year" award. Jennifer is now manager for national recruiting and supervises several employees.

Since Jennifer received Jesus Christ into her life, and she started living totally for Jesus, her life keeps getting better and better. God is truly awesome!

Let us examine Jennifer's life a little closer. Her maiden name was Jennifer Forrest. She was born in Lubbock, Texas January 28, 1975. Jennifer is currently 45 years of age. Her sister's name is Courtney.

Jennifer and her sister were raised by her father. Her mother left them and divorced her father when Jennifer was four years old. Her mom would see her on weekends.

Jennifer's father was brokenhearted when her mother left. He never remarried because he said one broken heart is enough. He drank heavily everyday but was a very hard worker and maintained a lifestyle of a functioning alcoholic. He kept the same job for over 20 years.

Jennifer states her father was amazing in the way he loved his kids. He loved his daughters, Jennifer and Courtney, and devoted his life to them. Jennifer states, "There was never a day I felt unloved, that is how I understand the unconditional love of our heavenly Father."

Jennifer's father did not go to church very much himself. He liked to watch the Sunday services on television. However, he would always take his daughters to Antioch Baptist Church in Lubbock every Wednesday and every Sunday. He would drop them off at church and pick them up when it was over.

Jennifer started smoking pot in 10<sup>th</sup> grade. She started running around with gangs. When she was 16, her sister's boyfriend gave her meth and Jennifer liked it. She started using the drug on weekends, then it was every day.

Jennifer went to prison three times which hurt all her family and most of all her three daughters: Leah, Macy, and Bailey.

Leah is her oldest daughter. She was born when Jennifer was a senior at Monterey High School in Lubbock, Texas. Jennifer dropped out of high school to have her baby. She went to school for pregnant girls and got her GED. Jennifer states that she was doing her best as a mom, but she knows she was not a good mother. Leah was moved around a lot among family members due to Jennifer's 18-year addiction to meth. Leah is currently 27 years old and has many struggles with her own addictions.

Jennifer's second daughter was Macy. Jennifer was in a very abusive relationship with Macy's father. Se states, "He tried to kill me twice, and I actually thought I was going to die." Jennifer was afraid if she kept Macy, her father would try to take her and possibly hurt her to. Jennifer gave her up at birth. She never even held her. Jennifer led a Christian couple adopt her and it turned out great for Macy. Macy graduated from Lubbock Christian University and was the chaplain of her dorm. Macy is currently married and is now a manager at Starbuck's. Macy has a great relationship with

God and her family Macy and Jennifer currently have a great relationship.

Jennifer's third daughter is Bailey. Bailey was born in 2005 when Jennifer was 30 years old and in federal prison. She went to a halfway house in Idaho for three months with her baby. Then her mother came and got the baby, and Jennifer went back to prison for another nine months. Bailey is currently 15 years old and has a great relationship with her mother, Jennifer. Jennifer has been clean and sober for the last 10 years.

Jennifer's third and last trip to prison was in 2010 for nine months.

This time it was a state prison. Jennifer had prayed with Stephen Canup with "Freedom in Jesus Prison Ministries" before her third prison sentence. Jennifer was given the option to stay in a faith-based dorm which she warmly welcomed. Stephen Canup asked her to make application to a "Road to Restoration" retreat given once a year for women getting out of prison and their families. She served nine months in prison and was then released. The last few months that she was imprisoned, she prayed to God every night to be delivered from the compulsion to do drugs. God delivered her from her 18-year addiction to meth.

Jennifer went to the retreat about a month or two after she was released. The retreat was great for her spiritual development.

Jennifer was invited to a "Freedom in Jesus Prison Ministries" ministry meeting. She remembers how kind and loving they were. They even helped put a new roof on her house. She wanted to be like them.

Jennifer was mentored by Stephen Canup with "Freedom in Jesus Prison Ministries" for the next year.

She became a team member with the "Road to Restoration" retreat ministry. They have a retreat once a year for ex-prisoners and their families.

This retreat is for 30 women and is held every February in Amherst, Texas at "The Ark."

Jennifer continues to be active in "Freedom in Jesus Prison Ministries."

She is happily married to her husband, Jeremy. They were married in 2013.

Jennifer had a setback in 2015 when her 4-year-old granddaughter, Kylee, was murdered by Kylee's father. The reason is not known, but Kylee's father had mental illness. It was devastating to Jennifer. Jennifer felt like her heart was shattered into a million pieces. She received counseling from "Freedom in Jesus

Prison Ministries" and the "Road to Restoration" ministry. She also received counseling from Pastor Gary Delay from Transformation Church. She was finally able to forgive this horrendous act.

As stated earlier, Jennifer has been delivered from her 18-year meth addiction and the mental illness it caused. She earned the "Employee of the Month" award on her first job after release from prison. Jennifer has been employed at "Wholesale Payments" for the last six years. She earned the "Telemarketer of the Year" award. Jennifer is now manager for national recruiting and supervises several employees.

Since Jennifer received Jesus Christ into her life, and she started living totally for Jesus, her life keeps getting better and better. God is truly awesome! She loves her husband and children and is successful at work. Jennifer is one of God's miracles.

**Jennifer Fortenberry can truly say, "Jesus, I trust in you."**

***Prayer:*** *Heavenly Father, I thank You for making deliverance from drugs and mental illness possible. Thank You for the miracle you performed in Jennifer's life. Thank You for restoring her family. In Jesus' name, I pray. Amen!*

Jennifer in 2010 before sobriety.

Jennifer in 2018.

Jennifer with daughter, Bailey, in 2019.

Jennifer with her husband, Jeremy, and daughter, Bailey.

Jennifer with husband, Jeremy, and daughter, Bailey, in 2017.

# Conclusion

## Free Indeed

***Therefore if the Son makes you free, you
shall be free indeed.***
*(John 8:36, NKJV, emphasis added)*

Each of the persons in this book were all set
free by Jesus. Some were in a physical prison,
and some were in a mental prison of darkness,
depression, loss of peace, drug addiction, and
mental illness.

Whatever is binding you, whether it is
depression, drugs, financial entanglements,
alcohol, a lengthy prison sentence, loss of
peace, divorce, or relationship issues, you can
be set free by Jesus.

The last part of this chapter will deal with how to become a Christian.

*Jesus said to him,* **"I am the way, the truth, and the life.** *No one comes to the Father except through Me.*
*(John 14:6, NKJV, emphasis added)*

Jesus is the way, the truth, and the life. Jesus is the only way to heaven. Jesus brings life not death. Jesus is the only way we can access our heavenly Father. All other ways, man's ways, lead to spiritual death which is an afterlife in a place called Hell.

**For God so loved the world that he gave his one and only Son, that whoever believes in him shall not perish but have eternal life.**
*(John 3:16, NIV, emphasis added)*

### The Dream of Heaven

*I had a dream about heaven on 5-29-2011. I had been thinking about heaven and reading about Christian near death experiences. I had already received Christ as Savior when I was 11 years old. "I dreamed I was standing at a narrow door which I understood to be the entrance door to heaven, but there was not a doorknob on the door. I was standing there trying to figure out how to get this door open, so I could get into heaven. I was getting worried that I may not be able to get into heaven. I was starting to get panicky. I said please God. Suddenly the door opened and a man in a white robe with brown hair and a brown beard and mustache (who I understood to be Jesus) looked at me very sternly and said "I am the way, the truth, and the life." Then He started smiling... the biggest smile I have ever seen and grabbed me tightly in a bear hug and pulled me through the door. I fell to His feet and then the dream was over."*

The message of this dream obviously is that Jesus is the only way to heaven. We must trust in Jesus Christ for salvation. In the Gospel of John chapter 3, Jesus tells Nicodemus that you must be "born again" to enter the kingdom of God. Born of the Spirit of God. This is when the Holy Spirit first takes up residence in the heart of the believer.

This is the first step that so many people miss. Without this step, often people go to church and soon become bored with church because they find no joy in it.

Sometimes, people go to church for years for various reasons but have no joy. They soon find every excuse not to go to church. When you receive Christ as savior, there is joy in going to church to worship God and have fellowship with other believers.

The following story is an illustration of God's salvation.

### The Story of the Little Boy and the Ship
*(author unknown)*

*There once was a little boy who lived near a lake. He decided to build a little ship. He worked on it every day after school. He finally finished it. Then every day after school, he would take the little ship down to the lake to play with it. He had so much fun playing with the ship. He looked forward to it every day. Then one day, he was playing with the ship at the lake and a gust of wind came. It filled the sails of the ship and the little ship took off across the lake. The little boy tried to catch it but could not. He was so sad for weeks. He missed the little ship he had made that was now lost. He missed all the fun they had together. One day while walking home from school, he saw his ship in a store window.*

*He was so excited. He ran into the store and told the store owner. "Mister, Mister, that's my ship, that's my ship. Give me back my ship." The store owner said, "Wait a minute, a man came into the store several weeks ago and sold me that ship. But if it is really yours, I will sell it to you for what it cost me." The little boy emptied all his pockets on the counter and said, "This is all I have." The store owner thought for a minute, then reached up in the window and took the ship down and gave it to the boy. It cost the little boy everything he had, but he was so glad to have the little ship back again. As he was leaving the store, the little boy held his little ship up admiring it and said, "You were once mine because I made you, now you are twice mine because I bought you."*

This is the story of salvation in symbols. The little boy symbolizes the heavenly Father. The ship symbolizes lost mankind. Our heavenly Father made us and enjoyed fellowship with us. We became lost through sin. We were bought back with the blood of His Son, Jesus. Salvation is offered to us freely after we repent.

The story of the prodigal son is in Luke 15:11-32. This story also contains symbols pertaining to salvation.

# The Parable of the Prodigal Son

**11** *To illustrate the point further, Jesus told them this story: "A man had two sons.* **12** *The younger son told his father, 'I want my share of your estate now before you die.' So his father agreed to divide his wealth between his sons.*

**13** *"A few days later this younger son packed all his belongings and moved to a distant land, and there he wasted all his money in wild living.* **14** *About the time his money ran out, a great famine swept over the land, and he began to starve.* **15** *He persuaded a local farmer to hire him, and the man sent him into his fields to feed the pigs.* **16** *The young man became so hungry that even the pods he was feeding the pigs looked good to him. But no one gave him anything.*

**17** *"When he finally came to his senses, he said to himself, 'At home even the hired servants have food enough to spare, and here I am dying of hunger!* **18** *I will go home to my father and say, "Father, I have sinned against both heaven and you,* **19** *and I am no longer worthy of being called your son. Please take me on as a hired servant."'*

**20** *"So he returned home to his father. And while he was still a long way off, his father saw him coming. Filled with love and compassion, he ran to his son, embraced him, and kissed him.* **21** *His son said to him, 'Father, I have sinned against both heaven and you, and I am no longer worthy of being called your son.'*

**22** *"But his father said to the servants, 'Quick! Bring the finest robe in the house and put it on him. Get a ring for his finger and sandals for his feet.* **23** *And kill the calf we have been fattening. We must celebrate with a feast,* **24** *for this son of mine was dead and has now returned to life. He was lost, but now he is found.' So the party began.*

**25** *"Meanwhile, the older son was in the fields working. When he returned home, he heard music and dancing in the house,* **26** *and he asked one of the servants what was going on.* **27** *'Your brother is back,' he was told, 'and your father has killed the fattened calf. We are celebrating because of his safe return.'*

**28** *"The older brother was angry and wouldn't go in. His father came out and begged him,* **29** *but he replied, 'All these years I've slaved for you and never once refused to do a single thing you told me to. And in all that time you never gave me even one young goat for a feast with my friends.* **30** *Yet when this son of yours comes back after squandering your money on prostitutes, you celebrate by killing the fattened calf!'*

*31* *"His father said to him, 'Look, dear son, you have always stayed by me, and everything I have is yours. 32 We had to celebrate this happy day. For your brother was dead and has come back to life! He was lost, but now he is found!'"*
(Luke 15:11-32 NLT).

The father in the story is symbolic of our heavenly Father. The runaway son is a picture of lost mankind. The father is so happy when the lost son returns home just as our heavenly Father is happy when we return to Him.

> *Jesus performed many other signs in the presence of his disciples, which are not recorded in this book.* But **these are written that you may believe that Jesus is the Messiah, the Son of God, and that by believing you may have life in his name.**
> *(John 20:30-31, NIV, emphasis added)*

Jesus is the Messiah, the Son of God. Jesus came that we might have life and life more abundantly.

It is hoped that everyone reading this book will give their heart and life to Jesus Christ. That everyone reading this book can now say, "Jesus, I trust in You!"

The salvation prayer is included below.

***Prayer:*** *Heavenly Father, help me to live a life centered around You. Help me make Jesus the center of my life. Jesus, I trust in You. Jesus is Lord of all. Thank You for the sweet honey of Your Word, the Bible. Create a clean heart in me, God. Renew a steadfast spirit within me. I call on Your name, Lord. I humble myself as I seek Your face. I ask You to show me what You have for me to do in Your kingdom. Help me to humbly glorify You and bring advancement to the Kingdom of God. I love You with all my heart, soul, and mind. Please help me to love my spouse, my children, and my neighbor as myself. I want to be Your child. Thank You for showing me how much I need you every day. I confess that I am a sinner, and I need forgiveness. I believe that Your Son, Jesus Christ, shed His blood and died for my sins and rose again on the third day. I repent of my sin. I now invite Jesus to come into my heart and life. Jesus, Son of God, I trust in You as my Lord and Savior, my Messiah! In Jesus' name, I pray. Amen!*

# Statement of Faith

I believe that one God exists in three persons: Father, Son, and Holy Spirit. Jesus Christ is the one and only Son of God who died for our sins and arose from the dead (1 Corinthians 15:1-8). The Bible is the inspired Word of God—a lamp unto our feet and a light unto our path (2 Timothy 3:16, Psalm 119:105). Every person has worth as a creation of God, but all have sinned and fallen short of the glory of God (Romans 3:23). Forgiveness of sins and the promise of eternal life are available to those who trust Christ as Savior and Lord (John 3:16). The church is the body of Christ on Earth, empowered by the Holy Spirit, and it exists to save the lost and edify the saved (Ephesians 4:1-16). Jesus Christ will one day return to Earth and reign forever as King of Kings and Lord of Lords (1 Thessalonians 4:13-18).

# Song

## "With God All Things Are Possible" (copyright 2020 by Mark Sundy)

*When I am in a pit of despair and hopelessness, Jesus, I will trust in You! With God all things are possible!*

*When addiction has taken my mind away, Jesus, I will trust in You! With God all things are possible!*

*When I am locked away, Jesus, I will trust in You! With God all things are possible!*

*When my enemies are pressing in, Jesus, I will trust in You! With God all things are possible!*

*When fear surrounds me, Jesus, I will trust in You! With God all things are possible!*

*When all my material possessions are stripped away, Jesus, I will trust in You! With God all things are possible!*

*When my children are taken away, Jesus, I will trust in You! With God all things are possible!*

*When I hear and see beyond this earthly veil, Jesus, I will trust in You! With God all things are possible!*

*When I feel worthless and unwanted and want to take my life, Jesus, I will trust in You! With God all things are possible!*

*With God all things are possible!*
*Jesus, I trust in You!*
*Jesus, I trust in You!*

## About the Author

 The author has written over 40 Christian inspirational and educational books. He also writes Christian song lyrics. The author currently resides in Ransom Canyon, Texas. He has a Master of Science in Nursing degree, Family Nurse Practitioner tract, from Hardin-Simmons University in Abilene, Tx. He has a Bachelor of Science degree in Geology from the University of Texas Permian Basin in Odessa, Tx. He has a Bachelor of Science degree in Nursing from Texas Tech University Health Sciences Center in Lubbock, Tx. He has a Associate in Arts degree from Howard College in Big Spring, Texas. He was employed as a Family Nurse Practitioner for 12 years before going into writing as a full-time occupation. He has two children and three grandchildren. He attends a non-denominational church. He has been on two medical mission trips to Honduras, two medical mission trips to Mexico, and a construction mission trip to Peru. He has also been involved in various Men's and Children's Ministries over the years.

## Contact Info
To write the author, please E-mail him at:
markmark_318@hotmail.com

# Other Books by Mark Sundy

### "MAN OF GOD: *Fulfilling Your Destiny as a Man*"

A Man of God is any man who delights in God's will and walks in the light of His truth, following in the footsteps of the Savior. This book will guide you in finding your own answers and becoming God's man!

### "GOD's MAN KING DAVID: A Giant Print 40 Day Devotional"

God's Man, King David, was a mighty warrior, a great king, and a man after God's own heart. This powerful, 40-day devotional will help you learn from what David did right as well as from his mistakes.

### "Dressed in Full Armor: A Powerful Praise Devotional Giving Glory to God"

We need to dress in the Full Armor of God to protect ourselves from the attacks of Satan. Isaiah 61:3 speaks of wearing a "garment of praise". This "garment of praise" could also be considered the "armor of praise". To dress in the full armor of God, you must put on your "garment of praise or armor of praise".

### "Mom's Old Fashioned Holiday Recipes: A Christian Cookbook"

This book is a collection of my Mom's and Grandmother's recipes for the Holidays plus a few other recipes from family and friends. Each recipe in this book also contains a Bible verse mentioning God as our ultimate source of food. This book also includes tid bits of cooking wisdom called wisdom pearls. Holiday recipes for Thanksgiving, Christmas, and New Year's Day are included. These are the Sundy Family Holiday Recipes.

### "FULL ARMOR: A Powerful Praise Devotional"

A different version of "Dressed in Full Armor". This version is longer and has study questions included with the text. This devotional is based on praise.

### "She is Strong and Graceful: Women Leaders of the Bible"

There were many godly women leaders in the Bible who were strong, graceful, and cheerful about the future. These leaders include Deborah the prophet and judge, Abigail the Wise One, Mary the mother of Jesus, Phoebe the Deacon, Esther the Queen, Tabitha full of good works, and Eve the mother of all living.

**"Generosity: Biblical Principles of Money Management"**
This book is all about learning biblical principles on how to manage the money God has given us.

**"Golden Pearls of Wisdom: Biblical Insight Into Your Problems"**
This book contains 14 golden pearls of wisdom to enlighten your mind and to help you understand the deep things of God.

**"Golden Pearls of Wisdom: The Sequel"**
This book is a sequel which contains 19 golden pearls of wisdom.

**"Kindness is Desired in a Man: The Kindness Principle"**
The Bible says to clothe yourselves with compassion, kindness, humility, gentleness, and patience. This book focuses on kindness. Isn't it amazing that you can put on kindness like you can put on your clothes? Like you put on your pants or shirt. Acting in kindness is a daily choice.

**"Unraveling the Mysteries: Biblical Enigmas Made Simple" Volume I**

The hidden mysteries of the Bible are there for us to search out. Proverbs 25:2 says "It is the glory of God to conceal a matter, but the glory of kings is to search out a matter" (NKJV). God conceals nuggets of truth, so his children can search them out. God has chosen to hide his mysteries from the wise and intellectual and reveal them to children. Two of those mysteries are included in this book. Those mysteries include the birth of the church, the bride of Christ, and how to become a part of the bride of Christ.

### "Unraveling the Mysteries: Biblical Enigmas Made Simple" Volume II

The hidden mysteries of the bible are there for us to search out. This is Volume II of "Unraveling the Mysteries". This book explores what it means to be "consecrated" or "set apart" for the purposes of God.

### "Rivalry: A Deadly Trap"

This book is about rivalry and its devastating consequences. Rivalry stems from the need to be accepted. This need to be accepted is rooted in our insecurities especially among siblings vying for the attention and favor of their parents.

### "Foundations of Joy: Learning to Live in Joy"

We must learn to live in joy. I rejoice in God my Savior! This book has been about learning to live in joy. It's about laying the foundations of joy which consists of three layers.

The foundations of faith, gratitude, and mercy. These are the roots of joy. Joy comes so much easier when you have faith in God. Joy comes so much easier when you are thankful and show gratitude to God no matter what circumstances you find yourself in.

### "Unraveling the Mysteries: Biblical Enigmas Made Simple Volume III"

The hidden mysteries of the bible are there for us to search out. This is Volume III of "Unraveling the Mysteries". This book explores the Mystery of Reconciliation.

### "Unraveling the Mysteries: Biblical Enigmas Made Simple Volume IV"

This book explores the "Mysteries of the Resurrection, the End Times, the Rapture, and the End of the World".

### "Outcast: Being Single in a Married Culture"

Have you ever felt like an "outcast"? This book is about being single in a married culture. The church world or the church culture is definitely and predominantly a married/family culture. This book is about coming to terms with being single, and it also discusses marriage and family. It also includes a discussion of divorce and the single-parent.

### "Surrender to Mercy: Living in Mercy"

This book discusses God's mercy, and how to live in God's mercy. The merciful man does good for his soul. Living in mercy is a choice that we make every day. Mercy is love and forgiveness and action.

### "Unraveling the Mysteries: Biblical Enigmas Made Simple Volume V"

This book explores the mystery of time. Part one of the book is man's perspective of time by some great men such as St. Augustine, Sir Isaac Newton, Albert Einstein, and Stephen Hawking. Part two of the book gives God's perspective of time as revealed by the Bible.

### "God's Benefit Plan: Psalm 103"

This book focuses on Psalm 103 which is 22 verses of pure gold. It is one of the most powerful chapters in the Bible. It addresses not only God's benefits for His children, but Psalm 103 includes a thorough description of God's mercy, and the purpose of God's angels.

### "Unraveling the Mysteries: Biblical Enigmas Made Simple Volume VI"

This book explores the mystery of "the fear of the Lord" or "the fear of God". What is fear? Is fear ever good? What is the difference between godly fear and ungodly fear? What does God say about fear? Is fear always bad? Are we supposed to be afraid of God? What happens in our brains and bodies when we are in a state of fear? These are good questions that are answered in this book.

Fear is mentioned 457 times in the New King James Version of the Bible. This fact alone is a very good reason to study the topic of fear. Fear is not always bad. The Bible tells us in Psalm 2:11 to "Serve the Lord with fear, and rejoice with trembling" (NKJV).

### "The Gift of Teaching: Open my Understanding"

This book is about the gift of teaching which is one of the gifts of the Holy Spirit. The "Great Commission" given by Jesus is usually talked about in the context of making disciples and baptizing them. However, this command is only the first requirement of the verse in Matthew above. Jesus also commanded His disciples to teach new believers to observe all things that he had taught.

### "Surrender to God's Mercy: An Easter Cantata"

This Easter Cantata contains six songs written by the author. The underlying message is about surrendering to God's mercy. God's mercy is shown in the Easter story by the crucifixion and resurrection of God's only son, Jesus Christ.

### "Unraveling the Mysteries: Biblical Enigmas Made Simple Volume VII"

This book explores the mysteries of the age of the Earth, the dinosaurs, and the unicorns. How old is the Earth? Does the Bible talk about dinosaurs? If not, then why not? Does the unicorn belong in mythology or did this animal once walk the Earth? This book answers these questions and more.

### "Unraveling the Mysteries: Biblical Enigmas Made Simple Volume VIII"

This book explores the mysteries of the Tree of Life, the Water of Life, and the Book of Life. What is the Tree of Life? What is the

Water of Life? What is the Book of Life? How can you make sure your name is written in the Book of Life? This book answers these questions and more.

### "Unraveling the Mysteries: Biblical Enigmas Made Simple"

This book is a 135-page compilation of the eight mini-book series "Unraveling the Mysteries".

### "Perfect Peace: Resting in God"

God wants us to have peace. Peace is mentioned 397 times in the New King James version of the Bible. St. Augustine of Hippo once said "Thou hast made us for thyself, O Lord, and our heart is restless until it finds its rest in thee." We are to trust in God enough to give Him all our worries and cares, and we receive peace in return.

This book is about having the perfect peace of God in our heart.

### "Strength in Unity: Becoming One"

There is strength in unity, and there is weakness in disunity. This book is about strength in unity. It is about becoming one through Jesus Christ. This book is about becoming unified in our marriages, families, businesses, churches and country by practicing two big biblical principles. The first principle is loving God with all your heart, soul, and mind. The second principle is loving your neighbor as yourself.

### "The Way That Seems Right to Man: Finding the Right Path to Eternal Life"

Are there many ways to heaven? What ways lead to spiritual life, and what ways lead to spiritual death?

Mankind believes his ways are justified and pure. According to mankind, there are many ways to heaven. Confucius had his way. Buddha had his way. Muhammed had his way. Hinduism has its way, etc., etc.! There have been many philosophies and religious sects through the centuries that all claim to have the right way to heaven.

This book discusses what seems right to mankind. It concludes with what the Bible says is the only way to heaven.

### "The Garden: Fellowship With God"

Why did God create mankind? What is fellowship? How do you have fellowship with God? How did God restore our broken fellowship? How do you love God? This book answers these questions.

Our heart seems to have a built-in cry to God. That is, a heart that cries out to be filled with the presence of God. Nothing else satisfies the heart of mankind. We fill ourselves with work, hobbies, relationships and are never satisfied until we find God and have fellowship with Him.

### "Mary: The Heart of a Mother"

What is motherhood? Who is the best example of motherhood? What are the traits of a good mother? What can we learn from the life of Mary, the mother of Jesus? This book answers these questions and more.

### "Gold Nuggets: A Treasure Chest of Wisdom"

What is the meaning of the term "gold nuggets" in this book? How do I recognize gold nuggets?

A gold nugget is biblical truth and wisdom. These gold nuggets of biblical wisdom are recognized when the Holy Spirit reveals them to you. Sometimes, you can read a scripture and not grasp the full meaning of it until the Holy Spirit quickens it in your spirit. This book is intended to help you acquire wisdom through the Bible.

### "Surrender to Mercy" 2nd Edition"

I originally wrote "Surrender to Mercy" two years ago. This book is a sequel that has been re-edited with additional material. This book discusses God's mercy, and how-to-live-in God's mercy.

### "Christian Growth: Spiritual Development"

You have given your life to Christ! That's great, but what do you do next? How does a person grow as a Christian? How does a person reach Christian maturity? This book answers these questions and more.

This book is written for all those who want to grow spiritually including those in prison and those in underground churches in countries where Christians are persecuted.

### "Hot Topics: Avoiding a Meltdown"

This book is about "Hot topics". These topics include: God's Sovereignty, Human Intimacy, the Sins of Sodom, and Christmas.

Have you ever wondered where God is when you go through hard times like the loss of a job, bankruptcy, and especially the death of a loved one?

The 1918 Spanish influenza pandemic caused millions of deaths. The 2019-2020 coronavirus pandemic is currently sweeping across the world causing thousands of deaths. If God is in control, then why do these things happen?

What were the sins of Sodom? Why did God destroy Sodom and Gomorrah with fire and brimstone?

What is the difference between human intimacy and human sexuality? How do we become intimate with our spouse?

Is Christmas Christian? Or is it just another over commercialized holiday for merchants to make more money? Is the birth of Jesus Christ actually on December 25th?

This book discusses these questions and more!

### "Warm Honey: God's Word the Bible"

Honey is symbolic for joy, prosperity, good health, God's blessings, and especially God's word—the Bible. God's word is sweet to the spirit and soul just like honey. Humans love physically sweet things like honey, chocolate, candy, ice cream, cake, etc. Our soul and spirit are the same way craving the sweetness of God's word.

This book discusses the sweetness of God's word.

## "The Center of All Things: Yeshua the Messiah"

*And He is before all things, and in Him all things consist.*

*(Colossians 1:17, NKJV, emphasis added)*

What is the center of all things? Or who is the center of all things? Who is Jesus Christ? We will answer these questions in this book.

St. Patrick had the right idea in his "Breastplate Prayer." Christ was the center of St. Patrick's life. Part of his prayer goes like this:

*Christ with me,*
*Christ before me,*
*Christ behind me,*
*Christ in me,*
*Christ beneath me,*
*Christ above me,*
*Christ on my right,*
*Christ on my left,*
*Christ when I lie down,*
*Christ when I sit down,*
*Christ when I arise,*
*Christ in the heart of every man who thinks of me,*
*Christ in the mouth of everyone who speaks of me,*
*Christ in every eye that sees me,*
*Christ in every ear that hears me.*

St. Patrick acknowledges Christ in everything in this prayer. Christ is the center of all things. There is a Latin term "summa summarum" which means highest, greatest, sum of sums, all in all. Jesus Christ is our "summa summarum." He is our "all in all" in the Christian life. Everything we do is for Jesus.

This book is about the center of all things, Jesus Christ.

### "Eschatology: The Study of the End-times"

*Now as He sat on the Mount of Olives, the disciples came to him privately, saying,* **"Tell us, when will these things be? And what will be the sign of Your coming, and of the end of the age?"**
*(Matthew 24:3, NKJV , emphasis added)*

What is Eschatology? The Merriam-Webster dictionary defines Eschatology as, "A branch of theology concerned with the final events in the history of the world or of humankind." Simply put, Eschatology is the study of the end-times.

There are many aspects of end-times theology. We will simplify and briefly discuss a few of them. This book discusses topics such as Dispensationalism, Covenant Theology, the Great Tribulation, Millennialism, the Second

Coming of Christ, the Resurrection of the Dead, the Great White Throne Judgment, and the Rapture. Complete books could be written on each of these topics. Our purpose is to simplify, so you can make up your own mind about each of them.

It seems as time goes on that these topics are made more and more complicated by seminary professors and church leaders. The important thing is that you make up your own mind and not let others tell you how you should believe.

### "Judges and Kings of Ancient Israel: Learning From History"

What can we learn from the Judges and Kings of ancient Israel?

The book of Judges in the Bible demonstrates the depravity of humankind. There are 12 judges listed in this book. There were cycles of disobedience, judgment, deliverance, and peace that repeated itself. There were 42 Kings of Israel and Judah.

We can learn much from the Judges and Kings of ancient Israel.

*Those who cannot learn from history are doomed to repeat it.*
*(George Santayana)*

Those that don't learn from history are condemned to repeat it.

This book is about the lessons we can learn from ancient Israel, so that we don't repeat the same mistakes.

### "With God All Things Are Possible: Jesus, I Trust In You"

This book contains four testimonials of God doing the impossible. Testimonials of God's redeeming power. Each of these men can truthfully say, "Jesus, I trust in You."

**All titles are available at Amazon.com online bookstore.**

Author 2<sup>nd</sup> from right-back (1979).

Author and children (2009).

Author's parents (1995).

Author's family (1977), Author 3rd from left.

Author with children and grandchildren (2015).

Author and his 3 grandchildren (2019).

Author 5 years old Christmas 1966.

Author 2020 mowing grass.

Author 5 years old on the left before church. September 1966.

Author 2020 (59 years old) in sunflower field.

Author in 2020 with children and
grandchildren.

Author with Mom and sister.

Author in 2020 grilling steaks.

Author 2<sup>nd</sup> from right in 2017 with brothers, Steve and Randall, and sister, Rita.

August 15, 2020 at Marriage Ceremony.
Pastor Mark Stripling, Author and wife, Sylvia.

Author and wife, Sylvia, at marriage ceremony
on August 15, 2020.

Author and wife, Sylvia, at marriage ceremony on August 15, 2020.